U. M. W.
1974

SPEAK THROUGH THE EARTHQUAKE

SPEAK THROUGH THE EARTHQUAKE,
  WIND, AND FIRE,
O STILL SMALL VOICE OF CALM!
              —JOHN GREENLEAF WHITTIER

SPEAK THROUGH THE EARTHQUAKE

RELIGIOUS FAITH AND EMOTIONAL CRISIS

ELIHU S. HOWLAND, M.D.

A PILGRIM PRESS BOOK
PHILADELPHIA

COPYRIGHT © 1972 UNITED CHURCH PRESS
ALL RIGHTS RESERVED

LIBRARY OF CONGRESS CATALOG
CARD NUMBER 79–185180
ISBN 0–8298–0229–0

FOR JOAN

CONTENTS

FOREWORD BY GRANGER E. WESTBERG   13
PREFACE   15
INTRODUCTION   21
CHAPTER 1   WHERE PSYCHIATRY AND THEOLOGY MEET   25
CHAPTER 2   IS GOD'S NEWS REALLY GOOD?   47
CHAPTER 3   FIVE UNSUCCESSFUL APPROACHES TO EMOTIONAL CRISIS   55
CHAPTER 4   CONSTRUCTIVE WAYS OF DEALING WITH EMOTIONAL CRISIS   73
APPENDIX A   PSYCHIATRY'S RESPONSIBILITY TO MEDICINE AND TO RELIGION   111
APPENDIX B   THE CLERGYMAN'S UNIQUE CONTRIBUTION TO HEALTH   121

SPEAK THROUGH THE EARTHQUAKE

FOREWORD

From the day I first met Elihu Howland to the time of reading this manuscript I have been impressed by his wholistic approach to the care of his patients. Despite his long period of preparation in both internal medicine and psychiatry he still felt the need to look deeply at the theological dimension of human suffering.

Twenty years ago there were few physicians who were willing to take the time to listen carefully to what theologians were saying. Dr. Howland listened. And he listened well—with a kind of openness and humility which contributes to true learning.

Now he has put down on paper some of his insights into faith concepts and has expressed them in ways only a person with his years of professional training and experience could. They are new, clarifying, and refreshing! This nontheologian has a way of making theology come alive. His insights will be of particular help to those in the healing professions to see more clearly the relationship between what a man believes about his nature and destiny and how this affects everything else that happens to him, especially the health of his spirit.

Dr. Howland is troubled by the current relationship between the clergyman and the psychiatrist; he says it is the psychiatrist who dominates. The clergyman is not just a junior partner, but "an extremely junior partner." He sees most of the conversation between the two as a monologue in which the psychiatrist tells the clergyman what to do in such stereotyped phrases as, "don't get in over your head," "know when to refer," and "remember you're not a psychiatrist." He questions whether any relationship operating on a street that is so exclusively one-way can be productive.

So he sets out to do something about it in this book which graphically demonstrates how important theology is in the healing process.

He is also troubled by the inadequacy and the confusion of clergymen. He sees them to be obsequious and apologetic about what they purport to believe and unconvincing about the power of faith because they have allowed themselves to be brainwashed by the more scientific-sounding jargon of psychiatry. But he does more than criticize the minister. He sets about to tell him, and anyone else who will listen, what he sees to be the great strengths of high religion and does it in a novel and convincing fashion.

The mood which he creates is one which sees psychiatry and religion existing not alongside each other, but as Paul Tillich would say, as "a relationship of mutual interpenetration."

Granger E. Westberg
Wittenberg University

PREFACE

It is common practice for an author to include his wife in his list of acknowledgments, usually at the end of the list. I am going to reverse the customary procedure and put my wife, Joan, at the head of my own list where I feel she belongs. It was a comment of hers that first led me to realize I had been overlooking the tremendous possibilities of the relationship between psychiatry and religion. Once I felt the call to work in this area, she sustained me in my conviction that I should try to make a statement about the importance of religious faith in the resolution of emotional crisis which both laymen and other professionals might find relevant and useful. Her unselfish arrangement of our family schedule was probably the biggest factor in my being able to complete this book as quickly as I did. Its dedication to her is a very small measure of my love and appreciation.

One logical way for me to learn about religion was to become more active in our own church. In the Brick Presbyterian Church in Rochester, New York I served as a deacon and also as an unofficial consultant to the church staff. My associations with Dr. David A. MacLennan, the senior minister, and with

Jean McDougall Brigham, the director of Christian education, were particularly rewarding.

In September 1958 I went to Dr. Oren Baker, who was then dean of the Colgate-Rochester Divinity School, and told him I wanted to spend a major part of my time collaborating with clergy in developing the relation between our two fields. Since I did not know how or where one might get started in this kind of work, I asked his advice. He wrote to Granger E. Westberg, a clergyman who held at that time an unusual dual appointment as associate professor in both the Divinity School and the Medical School of the University of Chicago. Dr. Westberg replied that at the moment there was no particular place offering this specific opportunity, but because of generally increasing interest along these lines he was hopeful that presently something would turn up.

That winter I first became aware of the work of Drs. Rollo May, Earl A. Loomis, Jr., and Thomas Hora. It seemed to me what they were saying pointed toward a very natural bridge between psychiatry and religion. I came to know these men, all of whom were helpful to me in a number of ways. It will be obvious to the reader that I have been influenced especially by the approach of Dr. Hora, which I have found very illuminating. His writings deserve to be known by psychiatrists and clergy even better than they already are, and by laymen as well.

In the spring of 1959, and again in 1960, Dr. Westberg invited me to Chicago to participate in a series of seminars he was leading for parish pastors. I was gratified to find he and I had many ideas in common about medicine, psychiatry, and religion. The opportunity to work with someone like this realistically did not exist in Rochester, or any other city I knew of. On the final morning of my second visit, as I was packing my suitcase, it suddenly struck me that perhaps I should seriously consider a permanent move to Chicago—even though I realized Dr. Westberg was in no position to provide me with an academic appointment, and the hazards of trying to establish myself as an independent practitioner in a big city where I was not known were undeniable. In spite of this, I had the persistent feeling that the key to what I was looking for might very well be in Chicago, and that with perseverance we might find a way for me to work either with Dr. Westberg or, through him, with other clergy in some new venture. I shared this idea with Dr. Westberg, who was most sympathetic to it and thoughtfully spent time with me during the next year investigating and weighing the possibilities and stark realities of the situation. The upshot was that I decided to take the gamble because I knew I would never have a chance like this again. In July 1961 we moved to the Chicago area.

Meanwhile, since 1952, the First Presbyterian Church of Evanston had been making a significant expansion of its pastoral counseling services. This was the joint idea of W. Clement Stone, a member of the congregation, and Harold Blake Walker, who was then the senior minister. Both of them recognized that emotional disturbance had become a major community problem in this country and also felt strongly that it was the church's responsibility to try to help. In a roundabout way, through my connection with Dr. Westberg, I made the acquaintance of Dr. Walker and some of the ministers, and in 1963 I was asked to join the church staff as part-time psychiatric consultant to the Pastoral Counseling Service. The Service continued to grow, and with it my position, so that since 1965 I have been working at the church full time. The generosity of Mr. Stone has made it possible for the Pastoral Counseling Service to carry on and for me to be part of it.

A feature which is unique to the Pastoral Counseling Service is that it is part of the church's total ministry; I am a staff member not only of the Counseling Service but of the church, and have been cordially invited by the other staff members to explore and become involved in other activities of the church in addition to counseling, particularly the department of Christian education. On occasion I have read the scripture lesson in the Sunday morning service, and have participated in a dialogue sermon and later in a "trialogue" sermon before the congregation. In the process of branching out in this fashion I have discovered that a number of barriers generally assumed to stand between psychiatry and religion actually do not exist. For all this and more I am grateful to these members of the church staff, past and present (in addition to Dr. Walker): John T. Mathison, Newland C. Roy, William H. Hudnut, Jr., Gary F. Skinner, Minnette M. Dummer, William Janssen, David A. Donovan, Robert A. Harris, Jr., Richard M. Alderson, Margaret E. Pijan, and Dr. Ernest J. Lewis, Dr. Walker's successor as senior minister, who has been a highly valued friend, spiritual leader, and supporter of the Pastoral Counseling Service; especially meaningful have been my associations with Herschel Allen, Jr., and James A. Guyer, our former counseling ministers, and with Fred Lewis, who is now our director of counseling.

I have much appreciated my opportunities to teach at various times with Dr. John W. Stettner at McCormick Theological Seminary and with Dr. Philip A. Anderson at Chicago Theological Seminary. Discussions and conversations with my seminary students have been enjoyable and stimulating, and have helped to sharpen my thinking in planning this book; outstanding among these students have been Karen L. Fink, Virginia R. Griffith, and Shirley W. Herman.

In 1967 and 1968 I served on the faculty of one of the Young Pastors' Seminars that are run regularly by the Presbyterian Church throughout the country. Dr. Robert A. Bonthius, the director of this particular seminar, exposed all of us to the problems faced by the "helping professions" in a big city—and in the process taught me an invaluable theological lesson which part of this book reflects.

Barbara Prasse's leadership of a seminar on the book of Ecclesiastes as part of the adult education program at the Winnetka Presbyterian Church awakened me to the significance of Ecclesiastes as a pathway to understanding the Christian message.

I am particularly indebted to those who read the initial version of the manuscript and offered sound criticisms and suggestions: Audrey Bard, Russell Becker, Perry LeFevre, Margaret Pijan, Edgar and Barbara Prasse, Birgit Shand, Elizabeth Stout, and Granger Westberg. In addition to everything else he has done for me, Dr. Westberg was kind enough to write the very gracious foreword. Dr. Pijan went over every word of the first draft with me before I showed it to anyone else, and passed on the second draft with equal care. She is a marvelously constructive critic with an unerring eye for inaccuracy, bombast, and other demonic forces that all too often rise from the depths to snare the struggling writer. As a friend with a truly phenomenal array of talents, Miss Stout was a great help in several ways. Dr. Becker provided the contact with the United Church Press, a publisher whose courtesy and efficiency I have found exceptional.

Jane Dyon typed the manuscript expertly. Mrs. Elizabeth Fitzpatrick, my secretary, was of considerable assistance with practical matters of correspondence.

Having elected to work on an interdisciplinary boundary, I have much appreciated the friends who have encouraged me in my decision to do this and also to write. Dr. Hora is one of these. Others I would like to mention in particular are the late Mrs. Lawrence W. Churchill, the late Dr. Edwards A. Park, Dr. L. Emmett Holt, Jr., Jane W. Mason, and Dr. F. Tremaine Billings, Jr.

It is clear that although this is not a large book, quite a number of people have contributed in one way or another to its production. And I would be remiss if I did not include our sons, John and Thomas, whose fair and honest questions about religion and its meaning and purpose have helped motivate me to try to put down in writing what is sometimes not so easily conveyed by the spoken word.

        Elihu S. Howland
        The First Presbyterian Church of Evanston
        Evanston, Illinois
        October 12, 1971

INTRODUCTION

In early September 1968, there appeared in the magazine *Presbyterian Life* a lead article by a layman writing under the pen name of "Jim Bryan" entitled, "What Should the Church Do About Mental Illness?" His fundamental question was: "What should be our Christian response and responsibility toward fellow Christians suffering from mental illness?" Bryan made no attempt to define the term "mental illness," but apparently assumed—and I think fairly enough—that his readers would understand what he was talking about. His contentions were that churches and their congregations are very important storehouses of abundant and effective help for such sufferers in a variety of ways. But he said that this help too often is not forthcoming because of the failure or misdirection of the church in its educational and healing ministry. This is shown by the seeming reluctance of churches to recognize the existence in their midst of problems of emotional disturbance.

"Bryan" had three recommendations to make toward providing more and better help. His first was for more open talk in churches about the needs of troubled people through sermons and discussion groups. His second was for the church staff and the congregation to surround troubled people and their families with love rather than to shy away from such people out of embarrassment. I was especially struck by his third recommendation, because to the best of my recollection I had never heard it made before, at least with such unmistakable clarity: the establishment of what Bryan calls "a distinctive Christian theology of mental health, developed on the basis of biblical insight," rather than on current schools of psychology, and asserting the permanent power of God alone to heal.

Bryan offers two statements in support of his recommendation for a theology of mental health. Secular psychiatrists, he declares, are now saying that ministers are well equipped to do the major part of psychotherapy, particularly in cases of depression. Admittedly, he does not tell us which secular psychiatrists are saying this, nor does he quote directly from any of them. He simply makes the assertion. What may have more impact on the reader is Bryan's second statement, that one of the most healing forces in the world is another human being who can listen with patience and love, and respond with what his faith directs at that moment. This, Bryan adds, is "therapy at its best." Note that the emphasis here is on what one's *faith* directs. The statement is clear and simple and does not suggest mysticism.

It is this kind of theology, based on biblical insight, which the present author (a psychiatrist who has worked for the last six years with the pastoral counseling service of a large suburban church) proposes to try to develop. Rather than use Bryan's expression, "a theology of mental health," I have chosen to present a theology of *emotional crisis*. The terms "mental health" and "mental illness" represent two ends of the same continuum, and therapists often disagree as to whether a particular pattern of behavior represents mental illness or not. The term "emotional crisis" indicates the existence of inner turmoil without attempting to categorize the individual as sick or well.

Three questions then immediately arise:

1. Is it legitimate and desirable to try to establish such a theology? I believe that it is, if for no other reason than the known fact that the greater number of people in emotional difficulty choose to go to a clergyman first for help. In addition, my experience in the church has made me aware that a number of troubled people who come for help have problems that are fundamentally theological and need to be understood as such. It will be presently shown that the approaches of certain psychiatrists lead us quite naturally and directly to religious ground. For all these reasons, the development of a theology of emotional crisis seems not only legitimate and desirable but imperative.

2. What right has a psychiatrist without any formal seminary education to try to develop a theology of this kind? Should not a theologian do this? The answer is that ideally a theologian is, of course, the one to do it; but to the best of my knowledge, so far no theologian has. Having acquired during my professional association with the church some measure of theological understanding, however slight, I feel emboldened to undertake this work with the hope that properly trained theologians may be moved to follow it up and improve upon it. I am particularly encouraged by

Paul Tillich's declaration that theology and psychology-psychiatry are not two realms sharply divided from one another, each with a special sphere, and that "the relationship [between psychiatry and theology] is not one of existing alongside each other; it is a relationship of mutual interpenetration."[1] The development of a theology of emotional crisis would seem to afford an unusual opportunity for this kind of mutual interpenetration to take place.

3. Must such a theology be purely Christian? The answer is that it need not be purely Christian. The frame of reference of this particular work will be largely Christian because of my own religious affiliation and experience. But I would not in any way seek to exclude its possible relevance to other religions.

---

[1] Paul Tillich, *Theology of Culture* (New York: Oxford University Press, 1959), p. 114.

CHAPTER 1
WHERE PSYCHIATRY AND THEOLOGY MEET

The first step in developing a theology of emotional crisis should be to state more clearly what we mean by "emotional crisis." An emotional crisis can be defined as a problem that is building up to a point where the individual feels his emotional balance is becoming precarious and seriously questions his ability to handle it much further.

Particularly common in an emotional crisis are anxiety, which may include some physical symptoms, and/or depression. The crisis may be precipitated by the possible or actual loss of someone or something cherished—even something intangible, such as an ideal—or a threat to oneself and one's own health or existence.

There is, of course, always the possibility that if the crisis is not relieved, the pressure on the individual may become realistically unbearable, with a resulting breakdown that may be physical or emotional, or occasionally both.

"Breakdown" is purely a lay term, so that what constitutes a "breakdown" is very much a matter of personal opinion. It is used here to mean a significant impairment of physical or emotional function, or both of these, to the extent that the person is unable to carry on any or most of his ordinary responsibilities. Sometimes it may include hospitalization. If the breakdown is emotional, there may be a time when it reaches the proportions of a psychosis—a state in which a person is having perceptible difficulty in distinguishing between reality and unreality in everyday affairs. In the event of a breakdown as defined in these terms, pastoral counseling, while still relevant to the situation, obviously needs to be integrated with the medical approach, including the psychiatric, that is indicated in the particular case. Prescription of medication and other measures within the scope of medicine are involved here, and a pastoral counselor should not try to take over the total or even major management of this kind of situation, or act without the knowledge and approval of a physician or psychiatrist except in most unusual situations where literally no other source of help is possible. Moreover, it is important for the pastoral counselor to keep in mind that the delusions of some psychotic patients may contain distorted religious material which he may have to play down or dampen, rather than trying to unravel them, because the patient's thinking is too disturbed.[1]

Further discussion of "breakdown" would be beyond the scope of this particular volume. And in fact it seems from what we have just said that there may be significant differences between a theological ap-

---

[1] However, one must also remember that the whole chaplaincy movement in state hospitals resulted from a psychotic episode in the life of the Rev. Anton T. Boisen, who during his psychosis felt a need to see a clergyman in order to maintain a natural and desirable sense of being in touch with God. (Anton T. Boisen, *Out of the Depths* [New York: Harper & Bros., 1960].)

proach to emotional crisis in which a breakdown has occurred and a theological approach to such a crisis where a breakdown has not occurred. Therefore this discussion of "emotional crisis" is limited to situations in which a breakdown has not yet occurred. The people in question are in some degree of emotional turmoil, often considerable, but are still capable of at least some measure of their customary function. And they are not psychotic, so that they are able to communicate the nature and extent of their distress understandably to others who are concerned and in a position to help.[2]

Among those who are concerned and sought out for help are clergymen and psychiatrists. In trying to be of assistance to troubled people, these two professional groups have been also attempting to find a common ground on which they might be better able to communicate with each other. This has not been easy.

Nevertheless, some progress has been made since the time that Freud spoke critically of religion as the "universal obsessional neurosis of mankind"[3] and declared that "it would be an illusion to suppose that we could get anywhere else what [science] cannot give us."[4] Indeed, it is known that Freud himself in his later years came to doubt his earlier claim that reason alone can be depended upon to save us.[5]

---

[2] A theology of emotional crisis in which a breakdown with psychosis has occurred may need to be the subject of a further and separate study.

[3] Sigmund Freud, *The Future of an Illusion* (New York: Liveright, 1949), p. 76.

[4] Ibid., p. 98.

[5] Percival Bailey, *Sigmund the Unserene* (Springfield, Ill.: Charles C. Thomas, 1965), p. 96.

Erich Fromm, an analyst with considerable knowledge of the Bible and of Eastern religions as well, is of the opinion that Freud was a highly ethical man not so much opposed to religion as to idolatry,[6] and that one task of both religion and psychoanalysis is to unmask contemporary forms of idolatry (for example, words, machines, the state, political groups, science, and so on). There is a good deal of truth in this. But Fromm emphasizes the uniting of religion and psychiatry (psychoanalysis) in the *negation* of idolatry.[7] He has nothing to say about how the two might come together in any *affirmative* statements about God. Without an affirmative statement as well as a negative one, one might wonder how the two fields could find a common ground on which to communicate with each other.

It is understandable that probably the most difficult step for the psychiatrist to take, because of the fact that he is currently trained as a scientist, is to admit into his frame of reference something frankly unscientific which emphasizes faith rather than reason. Nevertheless, as we shall now see, it has been possible for certain psychiatrists to move naturally, not only toward theological ground, but actually onto it.

J. F. T. BUGENTAL

A step in this direction has been taken by the psychiatrist J. F. T. Bugental. Admittedly, it is a limited step. In his technique, Bugental is essentially a psycho-

---

[6] Erich Fromm, *Psychoanalysis and Religion* (New Haven, Conn.: Yale University Press, 1959), p. 19.
[7] Ibid., p. 119.

analyst—which means that he has a preference for the couch rather than for face-to-face confrontation, and for an individual to visit him several times a week. This tends to limit his clientele to people of higher than average socio-economic position. To this author, Bugental's language seems a bit stilted, and authenticity as Bugental defines it resembles almost a commodity that one can buy, like a medication, rather than a characteristic or aim which must forever remain to some extent intangible.

However, Bugental does have more to say about authenticity than that. He grants openly that his thinking has been influenced by Tillich and by Thomas Hora, a psychiatrist with an unusual and refreshing point of view which will soon be brought to our attention.

Bugental's comment about mechanomorphic thinking in psychology is pertinent:

> That word "mechanomorphic" is a good one to characterize those views of human beings, that would devitalize human experience and extol the model of the machine. To those students, I would like to bring some hope that all psychology (or all psychotherapy) is not mechanomorphic and to arouse in them a bit of judicious rebellion.[8]

Later on he says (where he is not talking about drugs or mechanical therapy such as electro-shock):

---

[8] J. F. T. Bugental, *The Search for Authenticity* (New York: Holt, Rinehart and Winston, Inc., 1965), p. viii. Used by permission.

Psychotherapy is more art than science. This means that I cannot set down specifications which another therapist can take over intact and practice successfully, or even ones which I myself could use tomorrow with effectiveness.[9] . . . We give up hope of an orderly and completed system of thinking; but having given that up, we are begun upon an intellectual venture which has within it high excitement and genuine creative potential.[10] . . . Psychotherapy is not a healing process, but a philosophic venture.[11]

Religion has not been specifically mentioned, but Bugental has moved us from behavioral science to philosophy; and the next step could be to religion.

In this connection, Bugental has made an important contribution in emphasizing *tragedy* as an essential part of our being in the world, a part that our society, which seeks only comedy, has tried to deny. Tragedy, as one expression of the significance of our being, says that what we do matters; our choices may at times even make a difference between life and death. Furthermore, joy actually suffers from the suppression of tragedy, because it is less risky to spend our time and energy on amusements provided by others rather than give vent to the instinctive and joyous impulses which arise in the course of sharing between ourselves and others, or between ourselves and nature. Only through incorporating tragedy into our awareness of being,

---
[9] Ibid., p. 6.
[10] Ibid., p. 7.
[11] Ibid., p. 8.

Bugental says, can we regain joy.[12] The impossibility of assuring the outcomes of one's choices means that always there is the possibility of tragedy ensuing from any choice which one makes. Tragedy, therefore, is a part of man's nature which cannot be avoided.[13] As Bugental declares, too often a belief in God is a kind of deal the believer enters into with the Deity to guarantee him exceptional protection. When tragedy strikes, the believer then feels betrayed in his contract and accuses God of failing in his obligations. Such a use (or misuse) of religious faith, Bugental believes, is today largely rejected by many leaders in theology. Bugental's only specific reference pertaining to this is to Paul Tillich's *The Courage to Be*.[14] We shall have occasion to examine this crucial work of Tillich's a little later. At any rate, Bugental is not only emphasizing the inevitability of tragedy, but also seems to be implying that some constructive use can be made of it.

We can see here how Bugental has moved us from psychiatry through philosophy to the beginning of religious questions. What Bugental tells us about tragedy, and especially its constructive aspect, has a definite implication for religion. One example of this is George Buttrick's concept of Christ not trying to avoid pain, but walking clean through it and out the other side into the resurrection.[15]

---

[12] Ibid., pp. 151–53.
[13] Ibid., p. 164.
[14] Paul Tillich, *The Courage to Be* (New Haven: Yale University Press, 1959).
[15] George A. Buttrick, *God, Pain and Evil* (Nashville, Tenn.: Abingdon Press, 1966), p. 150.

VIKTOR FRANKL

Tragedy and suffering are not only part of the message but are quite essential to an understanding of the views of Viktor Frankl, the Viennese psychiatrist whose approach to people in emotional crisis has been powerfully influenced by his experiences as an inmate of World War II German concentration camps. Frankl's concepts, which carry us beyond Bugental, are formulated in what he calls "logotherapy," which he describes as if it were a sort of adjunct to psychotherapy as we are accustomed to think of it.

Logotherapy, derived by Frankl from the Greek *logos*, translated as "meaning" and also "spirit," has several distinguishing features. According to Frankl, there are "spiritual neuroses" (as contrasted with psychogenic neuroses) resulting from the failure of people to find meaning in life.

When Frankl speaks of "the meaning of life" he does not have in mind the meaning of life in general, but the *specific* meaning of an *individual's* life at a given moment. The meaning of life in this sense one can discover in three possible ways: (1) by doing a deed (in other words, achievement); (2) by experiencing something (for instance, a work of nature or of culture) or by experiencing someone through love; and (3) by experiencing *suffering*. It is the significance of suffering about which Frankl naturally has the most to say, because of having lived under appalling conditions in the prison camps, where individuals were constantly exposed to the real threat of fatal illness on the one hand or, if they were unable to work, being sent to the gas chamber on the other hand. In this ghastly situation every prisoner had occasion to wonder what the meaning of his life was, or whether indeed it had any. The majority were inclined to consider the meaning of their lives as directly related to the question of their own survival—that is, "If we don't survive, then all this suffering we are going through has no meaning." Frankl, however, realized that there was another way of looking at the situation: "If all this suffering we are going through has no meaning, then a life whose meaning depends on such a 'happenstance' as to whether one survives or not is not worth living." Therefore man should not ultimately ask what the meaning of his life is; he should instead recognize that it is he who is asked this question by life, and he can only respond by being responsible—that is, by doing all he can within the limits of the situation in which he finds himself.

This was a perception of unusual importance. It indicated to Frankl that not only does everyone have his own specific mission in life demanding fulfillment, but that it is also possible for everyone somehow to fulfill at least some measure of his mission, no matter how limited the circumstances are. For example, the manner in which a man faces death in a concentration camp serves a purpose, in that it can provide an example and inspiration for his comrades. It may be all he can do in that situation, but if he does it, his life has meaning. This "will to meaning" was of course an essential factor in maintaining the sense of purpose that enabled Frankl himself to survive. His own mission involved the completion of a book, the manuscript of which was snatched from him with a mocking expletive and destroyed by a guard when Frankl entered his first concentration camp. At that moment

Frankl knew that if he was to have any chance of living through whatever lay ahead for him, he would have to strike out his whole former life. In so doing he was able to resign himself to the destruction of his manuscript. He nevertheless found ways in the camps by which he could begin again patiently to outline and reorganize the work on scraps of paper. From these he has gradually produced, since the end of the war, not one but several books concerned with the problem of the meaning of life.

Obviously a concentration camp is not the only place where there are people who find their lives meaningless. They are all around us; they may at times even be ourselves. Here we should note particularly Frankl's statement that the true meaning of life is to be found in the world, rather than within man or his own psyche. The aim of human existence, he says, is *self-transcendence* rather than *self-actualization*. The latter can be attained only as a side effect of the former.

In these days there is much emphasis on the self—self-confidence, self-understanding, even self-actualization, which seems to have become the expressed purpose of a variety of ventures including certain of the so-called "sensitivity groups" and the use of drugs such as LSD, regarded by some as "mind-expanding." It is refreshing to be invited to transcend oneself in order to escape being completely preoccupied and drowned in oneself, and to have a look beyond, with the possibility that one may find the true meaning of one's life outside one's self rather than inside it. The self can, after all, become tiresome now and then, and can on occasion obscure our understanding as to what the aim of life really is.

Although Christianity cannot fairly claim to be the sole originator of the idea that self-transcendence should be our goal, there are nevertheless some echoes of Christian teaching in this declaration of Frankl's. Here it is interesting to observe in Frankl's explanation of logotherapy how he repeatedly contradicts himself regarding the relationship between logotherapy and religion.

He puts forward logotherapy (helping those who find no meaning in life) as therapy, that is, cure of the sick. Yet, in Man's Search for Meaning he says: "Existential frustration is in itself neither pathological nor pathogenic. A man's concern, even his despair, over the worthwhileness of life is a spiritual distress but by no means a mental disease."[16] This would appear to be a contradiction, in that what is offered is therapy, even though no disease is present.

A little earlier he states: "It must be kept in mind, however, that within the frame of reference of logotherapy [the word] 'spiritual' does not have a primarily religious connotation, but refers to the specifically human dimension."[17] In The Will to Meaning he asserts that "the essential difference between psychotherapy and religion is that one aims at mental health; the other, salvation."[18] Nevertheless, he says later on: "However, when a patient stands on the firm ground of religious belief, there can be no objection

---

[16] Viktor Frankl, Man's Search for Meaning (New York: Washington Square Press, 1963), p. 163. Used by permission of Beacon Press.

[17] Ibid., pp. 159–60.

[18] Viktor Frankl, The Will to Meaning (Plume Book; New York: New American Library, 1970), p. 143.

to making use of the therapeutic effect of his religious convictions and thereby drawing upon his spiritual resources," [19] which Frankl unhesitatingly does in the example that immediately follows, that of the rabbi who was helped by Frankl to understand that his sufferings were not in vain. In *The Will to Meaning*, especially in the last chapter, "The Dimensions of Meaning," there is an unmistakably religious tone.

Frankl is not an atheist or an agnostic. To anyone who has read or heard him, the conclusion is inescapable that Frankl has a religious conviction. The examples given above from his writings are only a few from an abundance of them. There is an unusually moving account of a spiritual communion with his first wife in *Man's Search for Meaning*. It took place when he was working on an early morning assignment and had no idea as to whether she was living or not (he learned subsequently that she had died in another concentration camp). A bird flew down, perched on a heap of soil that he had dug, and looked steadily at him.[20] When finally he and his fellow inmates were freed from the last concentration camp, he spontaneously knelt in the open field where larks sang and said: "I called to the Lord from my narrow prison and he answered me in the freedom of space." [21] On that day, in that hour, Frankl knew that his new life had started.

Frankl's thinking appeals to Christian Protestant clergy, a number of whom (for example, Tweedie, Leslie, Ungersma, and Paul Johnson) have worked with him in his clinic.

---

[19] Ibid., p. 188.
[20] Frankl, *Man's Search for Meaning*, op. cit., pp. 63–64.
[21] Ibid., p. 142.

To sum up: Frankl appears to have come to religious ground although he is reluctant to acknowledge it and states that he needs no theology. Nevertheless, he has provided a kind of theology of suffering that in many ways is consistent with Christian doctrine, and also a theology having *authenticity* (see Bugental, previous section), which genuinely attracts a large number and wide variety of people to read and to hear him. His seemingly contradictory stance on the relationship between psychiatry and religion is perhaps most clearly stated in *The Will to Meaning*: "Logotherapy does not cross the boundary between psychotherapy and religion, but leaves the door to religion open and leaves it to the patient whether or not to pass the door." [22] It is my belief that Frankl himself has already passed through the door and made it possible for other psychotherapists to follow him. Perhaps Frankl's seeming contradiction is because he considers religion as a personal matter, not to be confined within individual denominations. In any event, with Frankl we are at least at the gateway to religious ground, and probably already on it.

THOMAS HORA

The psychiatrist Thomas Hora has no hesitation in declaring that psychiatry and religion have a common meeting ground, and he takes us directly to it.

He reemphasizes Bugental's statement that man is confronted with vital decisions the outcomes of which he cannot predict, so that he is often tormented by fear and dread. In addition, Hora offers us guidance as to what to do when confronted with such fear and

---

[22] Frankl, *The Will to Meaning*, op. cit., p. 143.

dread. He points out that attempts to repress or deny dread do not prevent its existence, and that fighting against dread only aggravates it. Hora instead recommends the acceptance of anxiety and dread as inevitable conditions of life at certain times. Such acceptance leads to tranquil humility and a realistic attitude toward the world as it really is. He illustrates this beautifully by explaining that "life flows like a river and man has the . . . freedom to swim with the current or struggle against it in either direction, upstream or downstream. He will only find peace if he chooses to swim in harmony with the current." [23]

It is of the utmost importance to understand what Hora means by "swimming with the current." This statement is often misconstrued to mean being overpowered by the current and drowning, or hanging on with gritted teeth in the midst of perpetual and unbearable torment, or simply following popular opinion—in any case, being almost totally helpless. This is not what Hora is talking about at all.

In the first place, the man is not helpless; he is doing something—that is, swimming. He is doing the only thing he can do, but that is also all he needs to do. Nothing more is expected.

Moreover, he is swimming *with the current*, so that he is progressing. And since the current is supporting him, he is not self-sufficient or omnipotent, nor does he have to be. One can sense from Hora's words that the "current" is not merely that of popular opinion,

---

[23] Thomas Hora, "Psychotherapy, Existence and Religion," *Psychoanalysis and the Psychoanalytic Review*, Vol. 46 (Summer 1959), p. 95.

but something much more profound, beyond the limits of time and space. Returning for a moment to Bugental's comments about tragedy, this is of course one situation in which, in spite of everything, we discover that we are still able to swim and that we are sustained by the current simultaneously.

What Hora does mean is that in a time of emotional crisis, when we give up a struggle which serves no purpose, we become open to something else that does serve a purpose, and we eventually begin to see that we are not merely aware of this "something else" but are actually borne along by it, led by it in a direction that increasingly seems to be the right one. In Hora's own words, "In situations of . . . crises, man often becomes open to meet his God and fellow man." [24] It is plain that Hora has guided us quite naturally and without any awkwardness into territory that is definitely religious.

MARTIN BUBER

Becoming open to meet one's God and fellow man requires faith and trust, which are matters incapable of scientific proof; but one may nevertheless accept them. Martin Buber, the twentieth century's most unique Jewish religious thinker, says:

> The defensive man becomes literally rigid with fear. He sets between himself and the world a rigid

---

[24] Ibid., p. 98. There is a hint here of the importance of a *caring community* in situations of crisis—part of being open to meet God is the capacity to meet one's fellowman too. We shall have more to say about this presently.

religious dogma, a rigid system of philosophy, a rigid political belief and commitment to a group, and a rigid wall of personal values and habits. The open man, however, accepts his fear and relaxes into it.[25]

Most people make the natural mistake of immediately asking, "How do you relax in the midst of fear?" as though it were a procedure to be learned in mechanical or scientific steps. One slowly learns that it is not possible to understand faith and trust in this way.

Buber's "defensive man" has not accepted fear as a natural human reaction. He is confused by the fact that becoming open to meet one's God and fellow man has an anxiety-provoking aspect, because it means that one has to drop one's old defenses without any demonstrable proof as to what the outcome will be. He trusts no one but himself. He is determined to avoid fear at any cost, and as long as this is his main aim it is impossible for him to be open.

Buber's "open man" realizes that faith does not exclude fear. This is what makes it possible for him to "relax into his fear." No instruction is necessary as to "how to do it." It happens naturally and gradually through experience.

PAUL TILLICH

In his concluding sentence in *The Courage to Be* Paul Tillich asserts that "The courage to be is rooted in the God who appears when God has disappeared in

---

[25] Maurice S. Friedman, *Martin Buber: The Life of Dialogue* (Chicago: University of Chicago Press, 1956), p. 136.

the anxiety of doubt." [26] That is to say, the God who vanishes in the anxiety of doubt is apt to be a false God constructed chiefly from our own rigid preconceptions about what or who we think God should be, preconceptions which only interfere with our awareness of the presence of the real God. Tillich then leads us further into an area so uncomfortable for us that we seek to avoid it:

> It is our destiny and the destiny of everything in our world that we must come to an end. . . . Whenever we are shaken by this voice reminding us of our end, we ask anxiously what it means that . . . we come from the darkness of the "not yet" and rush ahead towards the darkness of the "no more"? When Augustine asked this question, he began his attempt to answer it with a prayer. And it is right to do so because praying means elevating oneself to the eternal.[27]

He explains what the eternal means, and gives two common misconceptions about it: (1) Many people try to put "the expectation of a long life between now and the end." (2) Many other people realize that this is deceptive and "hope for a continuation of this life after death. They expect an endless future in which they may achieve or possess what has been denied them in this life." They replace "eternity" by "endless future." "*But endless future is without a final aim;*

---

[26] Tillich, *The Courage to Be*, op. cit., p. 190.
[27] Paul Tillich, *The Eternal Now* (New York: Charles Scribner's Sons, 1963), pp. 122–23.

it repeats itself and could well be described as an image of hell." [28] (Italics are mine; if one stops to think about this, one sees how absolutely true it is.)

Tillich goes on: "This is not the Christian way of dealing with the end. The Christian message says that the eternal stands above past and future. . . . There is no time *after* time, but there is eternity *above* time." [29]

Eternity is above not only time but above human comprehension also, as Tillich illustrates:

> We ask about life after death, yet seldom do we ask about our being before birth. But is it possible to do one without the other? The fourth gospel does not think so. When it speaks of the eternity of the Christ, it does not only point to his return to eternity, but also to his coming *from* eternity. "Truly, truly I say unto you, before Abraham *was*, I *am*." [30]

The Christ belongs to a dimension which human reason alone can never expect to understand.

It may be quite disturbing to many people, including a number of very intelligent people, to admit that there may be, or perhaps even is, a dimension forever inaccessible to human reason. Admittedly, part of the task of science is to maintain some degree of skepticism about mysteries, and to keep nibbling away at them to see whether they are truly mysteries or not. But if in this way we manage to expose portions of the

---

[28] Ibid., p. 125.
[29] Ibid.
[30] Ibid., p. 126.

fringe for what they really are, and a central core of true mystery remains, what then? Are we to give up all hope? Buber, for one, would say not. He would advise us to relax into our fear, and then we will discover the truth that will comfort us and make us free. Tillich does not use Buber's identical words, but the message is the same:

> "I am the beginning and the end." This is said to us who live in the bondage of time, who have to face the end, who cannot escape the past, who need a present to stand upon. Each of the modes of time [past, present, and future] has its peculiar mystery, each of them gives its peculiar anxiety. Each of them drives us to an ultimate question. There is one answer to these questions—the eternal. . . . He who was and is and is to come, the beginning and the end. He gives us forgiveness for what has passed. He gives us courage for what is to come. He gives us rest in His eternal presence.[31]

Tillich says in essence: "You cannot prove God, but you can always trust in him." If one accepts this possibility, one finds that it is not as incredible as it seemed at first glance. *Faith and doubt do not necessarily contradict one another.* Again, Tillich: "Faith includes the courage to take the risk of the uncertain and unprovable upon itself; faith says 'Yes' in spite of the anxiety of 'No.'"[32]

---

[31] Ibid., pp. 131–32.
[32] Paul Tillich, *Biblical Religion and the Search for Ultimate Reality* (Chicago: University of Chicago Press, 1955), p. 61.

What Buber and Tillich are telling us is that there may come a point in human crisis beyond which reason alone cannot prevail, and we see that faith inevitably includes doubt. Yet it is here, on this uncertain but unmistakably religious ground, that we may feel God's guidance perhaps for the first time in our lives.

Two conclusions can be made from all this:

1. *It is possible to proceed by means of faith across territory where reason alone may have no guidelines to offer.* There is always meaning to be found in life, always something one can do, no matter how bad the situation is. While this last statement could not be called irrational, it is "arational," that is, a conclusion arrived at by faith rather than by pure reason. For although one may believe it, one cannot prove it beyond question. This is a declaration of faith in spite of doubt.

2. *Through faith in a higher power it becomes not only possible but even legitimate for us both to accept for ourselves and to make to others certain promises which reason alone may not be in a position to make.* The Christian religion will be used to illustrate this, because we are better acquainted with it than with other religions, though others may well be able to provide just as many equally valid examples. The Bible, of course, is one rich source of promises going beyond the scope of reason, and it would be difficult to find a single instance in which, when biblical teaching has been consistently followed and eventually understood by a person in emotional crisis, the promises made to him or to her by God have not been fulfilled with relief of the crisis in some way. However, since it is very easy to misinterpret these promises, it is es-

sential that we seek to understand as best we can just what it is that God has promised. This could be considered patronizing in that it may appear to be interpreting the Christian faith to a number of people who actually know much more about it. This, however, is not the intention at all, as will presently be seen.

CHAPTER 2

IS GOD'S GOOD NEWS REALLY GOOD?

Comprehension of the nature and extent of the divine promises made to us by Christianity begins with what is known as the good news of Jesus Christ. The simplest statement of this is that God loves us without our having done anything to deserve it, and that he demonstrated his love for us in the highest possible way, by entering our world in the person of his son Jesus Christ, who, although divine, lived as a man among other men.

It is essential for us to understand as clearly as we can what Christ did. There were many witnesses to what he did, and their accounts of what happened were passed on by these witnesses to others who ultimately recorded them in the New Testament, chiefly in the four Gospels. Primarily, Christ taught the love of God and of one's neighbor. In so doing, he permitted himself to be crucified by his enemies, who were both jealous and afraid of him. As the Son of God, he knew it was necessary for him to do this in order that God's purpose of reconciling our world to himself be achieved.[1] In other words, he recognized the implica-

---

[1] Reconcile = to restore to friendship, harmony, or communion. Here once more is the suggestion that commitment to Christ includes involvement in a caring *community*, which is also one of the points emphasized in "Jim Bryan's" article referred to in the Introduction.

tions of the crucifixion, which man alone could not understand. As man, at the time of the crucifixion he did as much as man could possibly do, and no more. He did not try to avoid carrying out God's will, and he did not attempt to save himself by a miracle. Then he rose again from the dead, thereby demonstrating that God ultimately triumphs over all evil and that God's reconciling love for us is constant.[2]

The most remarkable aspects of God's love are that *it is not forced upon us, but is freely available to anyone who truly wishes to receive it;* and that *this is God's doing and not ours.* Obviously we should do all we can in any situation in which we find ourselves. But what is of primary importance is *not what we can do for ourselves, but what God has already done for us.* This is a very heady message, which requires time and thought to assimilate; and we shall come back to this again.[3]

---

[2] The best way to get a conception of Christ as man and God simultaneously is to read the New Testament. There are a number of versions of the New Testament, and one is free to choose whichever he prefers: the *King James Version;* the *Revised Standard Version; The New Testament in Modern English,* J. B. Phillips, trans. (New York: Macmillan, 1958); the *New English Bible* (New York: Oxford University Press, Cambridge University Press, 1961); and the popular edition *Good News for Modern Man* (New York: American Bible Society, 1966).

[3] In the New Testament, God is frequently spoken of as the Trinity or the Three in One, namely the Father, the Son (Christ), and the Holy Spirit. In the New Testament, the Holy Spirit is probably mentioned most specifically on the occasion of Pentecost, when it is stated that the Spirit made it possible for the disciples to be understood by all listeners who were present, in spite of the natural language barriers that existed.

However, when we speak of the good news of Jesus Christ, a question arises immediately which demands an answer: Can we in all fairness proclaim the good news of God's reconciling love in a world in which we know there is so much suffering? The answer is Yes.

There are two alternatives to this belief:

1. The world exists by chance, there is no power we can call God, and life is absurd. Some individuals, including the late Albert Camus, have accepted this idea; but on the whole man rejects it, as Frankl has, for example.

2. God decides everything in the world and man is like a puppet on a string with no responsibility of his own at all. There is no real meaning to a life of this kind either, and from our own experience we know that this is not how the world is; we have both freedom and the responsibility that goes with it.

The fact of the matter is that a free world is not necessarily a fair world—and it is this fact that we must realize while seeing whether there is any way of reconciling it with the message of the good news that God ultimately triumphs over all evil.

We can find in our own life experiences many instances of what we consider, often rightly, injustices to ourselves and to others. What makes it harder is that this state of affairs has obviously persisted throughout all of history. One of the best expressions of the entire dilemma is set forth in the Old Testament book of Ecclesiastes, the Preacher. The problems confronting him have been quite rightly compared to the uncertainties and despairs of our own present day.

The Preacher begins by pointing out a number of discouraging and even crushing observations he has made in his lifetime. He says that all human courses seem "vain," by which he means useless. In his own words, "Vanity of vanities; all is vanity (Eccles. 1:2, KJV).... There is no new thing under the sun.... There is no remembrance of former things ... [nor] of things that are to come with those that shall come after (1:9–11, KJV)." Man cannot create anything that is new or permanent, or that in itself gives any lasting pleasure (2:11). People are never satisfied with their possessions (5:10), but always want more.

Furthermore, there is no justice. Wickedness not only exists in the world in the midst of righteousness (3:16), but at times definitely flourishes. Just men may die in their righteousness while the wicked survive in their wickedness (7:15). The righteous and the wicked alike are equally exposed to unpredictable disaster (9:2); and the presumed truth of a very old teaching, fragments of which still seem to linger even in the present, was actually exploded centuries ago by the Preacher's honest statement that he saw that the race is not, after all, to the swift, nor the battle to the strong, nor bread to the wise, nor riches to the intelligent, nor favor to the men of skill; but time and chance happen to them all (9:11).

What may be even more disquieting to us is that the Preacher seems, at least, to have little to tell as to what we can do about any of this. Indeed, he raises more questions than he appears to answer; and while he does have some answers for us, they sound hardly reassuring:

Times change, and we must be prepared to alter our actions and behavior depending on what the situation calls for (3:1–8).

It is God's purpose that we should "eat and drink," and enjoy the good of our work. The importance to the Preacher of doing these things is quite evident because he repeats this three times (2:24, 3:13, 9:7). We should also, if we are married, live happily with our spouses. But the only reason the Preacher gives as to why we should do all this is that the opportunity will not last forever and when we die it will be too late.

It may be additionally depressing to learn that the Preacher considers sorrow as better than laughter; in fact he even implies that laughter is one sign of a fool (7:2–6). A sense of humor is almost essential to the joy of living, but the Preacher is speaking here of *incessant* laughter, with the unwillingness to admit the existence of sorrow and the possibility of some constructive use of tragedy.

We are not surprised to be told that patience is preferable to pride (7:8). Wisdom, although not actually defined, is particularly recommended (7:11–12; 9:16–18), but in some moderation, because to be either too righteous or what the Preacher calls "overwise" he declares is self-destructive (7:16).

These scraps of advice at first perusal are apt to strike us as not really enough to base our entire lives on. Our crowning disillusionment may be at the very end of the book when the Preacher, having summed up these few points, comes out with the ultimate conclusion that man's whole duty is to fear God and keep his commandments. Here our total frustration may burst forth: "So what's new about this? This is the same old stuff that's been pushed at us since time immemorial, and it's nothing but words; it doesn't mean a thing. Promises, promises, just as long as we keep God's commandments. None of the promises have come true, and there's no indication that any of them ever will; but in spite of that, all that Ecclesiastes tells us is simply to go on keeping God's commandments, without any explanation as to why. How can there possibly be any meaning to a life as empty as this?"

But here Viktor Frankl's spiritual message is helpful, because he reminds us again that this is the question life is asking of us, not we of life. It is the way in which we respond to the question that we ultimately find the meaning for which we are searching. In addition, Christ offers us more comfort than Ecclesiastes in assuring us of God's love. Where the Preacher says "Fear God," Christ would say "Love God." But in either case the world is still the same, full of danger and injustice as it always has been. It is in this kind of world that we live and must find a reason for living. Because we fail to recognize this, we may misinterpret Christ's teaching and be consequently surprised and disappointed when miracles do not happen and our prayers are apparently not answered. If the world were not truly as uncertain and full of suffering as the Preacher describes it, a ministry to people in emotional crisis would be unnecessary, let alone a theology of emotional crisis. In fact, we humans are such perverse creatures that if suffering were not part of our world we would probably be incapable of loving God at all. As it is, when we face the matter directly we can see that we neither fear nor love God with any semblance of consistency, nor do we truly keep his commandments.

An understanding of the book of Ecclesiastes is essential for an understanding of Christian teaching. We professed Christians may be inclined to forget our indebtedness to the Old Testament, and that our so-called Christian heritage is actually Judeo-Christian. Actually, when we accept the existence, and even at times the spread, of insecurity, sin, peril, and suffering as an undeniable part of our world, we are in a better position to understand the importance of Ecclesiastes' final admonition to keep God's commandments. And we also can comprehend and experience more fully the great joy and freedom of the good news of Jesus Christ if, paradoxically, we acknowledge the limitations of the world in which we receive the good news. The words of Robert Bonthius, a nationally respected Presbyterian clergyman, seem relevant here: "We cannot by ourselves change the course of history. We can only bear witness." [4] This is not a message of discouragement; quite the contrary. Bonthius is encouraging us to bear witness because that is the way in which the good news comes to us. It is when we try to change the world by ourselves that we are doomed to failure.

We are now in a position to begin to see how the good news cannot only sustain a person through an emotional crisis but cause some good to come of the experience.

---

[4] From a personal communication.

CHAPTER 3
FIVE UNSUCCESSFUL APPROACHES TO EMOTIONAL CRISIS

The person in emotional crisis may choose to struggle with his problems alone, or he may seek help from family, friends, or a trained professional, or sometimes all of these. In any case he will try to cope with his problems in various ways. Often he becomes frustrated and discouraged because a number of these ways of trying to resolve the problems inevitably fail. They are in vain, as Ecclesiastes would say. Another way of putting it is that these methods fail because they are not primarily based on faith and trust beyond oneself.

We must remember, however, that it is all too easy to criticize people who have sought to solve their problems in such a variety of ways, because most of us, whether we realize it or not, have at least tried some of these ways ourselves. We learn by experience that it is one thing to be outside a situation where one can freely comment and criticize, and quite another to be in the midst of such a situation personally, when we discover that our perceptions of it are considerably different from what we had assumed previously. Nevertheless, we believe that the attempts of the person in emotional crisis to deal with his problem in the ways which follow are not sound—for himself, or those with whom he is most closely concerned.

1. SELF—SUFFICIENCY

We have already dealt with this in our preceding comments about the work of Viktor Frankl, who says that the true meaning of life is found in self-transcendence rather than in self-actualization, let alone self-sufficiency. But many people still cling to the idea that self-sufficiency is the goal of life; and current popular media often support this idea.

Perhaps the most beautiful and moving declaration in support of self-sufficiency is the poem "Invictus," by William Ernest Henley. Henley was hospitalized for twenty months because of tuberculosis, during which time one of his feet had to be amputated. In spite of all this, he eventually became well. "Invictus" is his cry of defiance, very likely in one of his blackest moments of illness:

> Out of the night that covers me,
> Black as the Pit from pole to pole,
> I thank whatever gods may be
> For my unconquerable soul.
>
> In the fell clutch of circumstance
> I have not winced nor cried aloud.
> Under the bludgeonings of chance
> My head is bloody, but unbowed.
>
> Beyond this place of wrath and tears
> Looms but the Horror of the shade,
> And yet the menace of the years
> Finds, and shall find, me unafraid.
>
> It matters not how strait the gate,
> How charged with punishments the scroll,

> I am the master of my fate:
> I am the captain of my soul.[1]

We may be so fired temporarily by the impact of the man's courage, inspiration, and choice of words that we may overlook the fact that this head-on attack, or resistance, which may have some value in a physical illness, is not in itself enough to sustain a person who is in a severe degree of emotional turmoil. There are two reasons for this. It accentuates and focuses on the fearful and painful aspects of the situation, which only serves to remind the person of what he is all too conscious of as it is. It also focuses on the self, and thereby commits one to a course of action which one already realizes cannot succeed. If there is one thing that an individual in emotional crisis knows, it is that he is neither the master of his fate nor the captain of his soul. He is in desperate search of an answer to his problem; he cannot find the answer within himself, nor does an answer seem to be coming from any source with which he is familiar. To him, it is not the words of Henley but those of Blaise Pascal that most accurately describe how things are in emotional crisis: "The eternal silence of these infinite spaces frightens me."[2] In such a crisis one begins to perceive that he is the plaything of vast forces far beyond his control, and that he is not omnipotent or self-sufficient.

Working with troubled people reveals a tendency

---

[1] "Invictus" from *Poems by William Ernest Henley*. Used by permission of Macmillan London and Basingstoke.
[2] Blaise Pascal, *The Thoughts of Blaise Pascal* (Dolphin Books; New York: Doubleday), p. 277.

not uncommon among professed Christians, including even some clergy, to assume that a Christian is not supposed to experience anxiety or doubt, or at least not very much. If he does, it means that he is a "bad Christian." This, of course, is not true at all. In such instances there has been an inadvertent confusion of Christianity with self-sufficiency, and it becomes very important to clarify this point as soon as possible. The religious man is still a human being, and has just as much capacity for anxiety and doubt as the non-religious man. Failure to realize this may lead to despair and to unfortunate decisions. We shall have more to say about this later on.

One weakness in the notion of self-sufficiency is that the concept of the caring community is entirely left out. The implication seems to be, "If you're self-sufficient, who needs a community?" But anyone in emotional crisis is definitely in need of a community. The sense of isolation experienced in such a crisis can be devastating—the feeling that no one else understands, no one else would feel the same way, or even if he did, it would not bother him very much. Anton Boisen has spoken of this sense of isolation,[3] also Hobart Mowrer[4] and many other commentators. The troubled person needs to be understood,to realize that he is not alone, and to feel in communion with others. It is paradoxical that when one feels most isolated, he may actually be sharing in a universal predicament. This happens at

---

[3] Anton J. Boisen, *Out of the Depths* (New York: Harper & Bros., 1960).

[4] O. Hobart Mowrer, *The Crisis in Psychiatry and Religion* (Princeton, N.J.: D. Van Nostrand Co., 1961), p. 25.

times to many of us and could happen to anyone, especially when we are least prepared for it. The faith of others sustains us, even though we may not be aware of this at the moment, and may not perceive until later on how much it has helped.

2. "THE FALL OF VALOR"[5] OR "QUITTING"

Here we have to be sure that we know what we are talking about, because "quitting" is a loaded word, which can imply disgrace, or can be used casually to mean disengaging oneself from one venture in order to undertake another which may be more worthwhile (for example, "I quit banking because I thought I would do better to go to law school"). In this instance, the previous experience in banking is not necessarily depreciated simply because of the decision to do something else. The past experience may even be useful to the person in his new undertaking. The decision to change is made because the person feels that he can do more people more good by shifting to a situation in which he feels he has more genuine interest and for which he may have more aptitude.

This is to be differentiated from the situation from which one tries to remove himself purely to avoid pressure and anxiety. Melville's phrase, "the fall of valor," is a more accurate description of this kind of critical decision than "quitting," but even there one must be prepared for differences of personal opinion. One of the problems of living in our world is that a person must sooner or later decide what he must do, and then

---

[5] Herman Melville, *Moby Dick* (New York: Random House, 1930), p. 166.

do it. He should be prepared for the possibility, and even likelihood, that there will always be some who will interpret his action as "not facing reality," or just "being difficult."

This problem is complicated by contemporary ideas of the importance of success as opposed to failure, and winning in contrast to losing, where an individual becomes uncomfortably aware that he may "lose" according to most conventional standards, in spite of his having done the best he can. We forget that there is, after all, such a thing as a "moral victory." In this connection it is important to recall that the modern Olympic Games were founded by Baron de Coubertin on the principle that it is not as important to win as to participate and do one's best. This idea somehow reminds us of the advice of Ecclesiastes, and it is easy in modern times to lose sight of this kind of teaching.

"Quitting" used in the sense of a "fall of valor" means a deliberate choice to run away from a threatening situation which it would have been possible at least to face and attempt to deal with in a more constructive manner. "Quitting" is apt to carry with it the implication not only that the quitter is a coward, but that the menace confronting him was relatively slight and should not have made him feel very anxious. In a great many cases this latter notion is totally fallacious. The realization that one is not self-sufficient, combined with the grim specter of possible or even probable failure to master the challenge at hand, realistically generates an anxiety so intense that it is almost unbelievable. But, even so, the challenge can often be met and the risk taken. The tragedy occurs when the individual turns aside instead and thereby acts at less than his full potential for the sake of self-preservation.

There may be occasions, however, when a person does not wish to go that far, because he fears that if he were to behave so obviously he would lose the respect of his friends. In some cases it may be possible for the person to get around this difficulty by pseudo-participation at a level definitely lower than his true ability, followed by the claim that he really did his best and could have done no more. Because it is usually impossible to disprove such a claim completely, the individual may have a good chance of convincing others that he is speaking the truth, especially since people are generally reluctant to believe that a friend of whom they are genuinely fond would do such a thing as quit in a crisis. Indeed, the act of quitting may often be more distressing to the observer who suspects the true state of affairs than to the person involved, who frequently experiences not guilt but an immense relief of tension because he has found a solution which eliminates the crisis without personal risk and still allows him to remain socially acceptable.

One individual, who may not have realized the full significance of what he was saying, declared, "I enjoyed the *exquisite pleasure of quitting*" (italics mine). The man was a splendid competitor, who had never before left a situation of challenge and conflict purely for his own personal comfort. This was his quite spontaneous reaction to a new experience, where the pressure of responsibility had been lifted by his decision.

Competitive sport is one obvious situation where

tension is high and where pseudo-participation without detection may be possible, so that the temptation is great. The account of a client illustrates this:

> Once I saw a very good friend of mine quit in a track meet. You know what I mean: he ran the race, and yet he didn't really run it. He just wasn't trying. It was one of the most awful things I've ever seen. It was the deciding event of the big meet at the end of the season. We needed a second place to win, and he came in last—a bad last, way behind the others. It lost the meet for us, and broke an undefeated streak we'd had going for several seasons. And it was more than just "rah-rah" stuff. Our coach was a great teacher, and he saw sports as a way of preparing young men for life.
>
> I'll grant you it was a hot spot for my friend to be in, especially since he hadn't expected to run that event. But we were in a jam, and he was fresh and rested compared to the others in the race, so our coach called on him. Besides, I'd seen him run that particular distance in time trials before, and I knew what he could do. He could have gotten second easily if he'd put out. But I knew him well enough to tell that he wasn't putting out. His legs were moving, but there wasn't any real drive to his stride. He must have decided when he was called on, even before the race started, that he was going to coast and blow it.
>
> I was standing beside the finish line when he crossed it. He came up to me and said, "I couldn't help it. I did the best I could." And then do you know what I did? I said, "I know you did," and I

shook hands with him. He started back to the bench and I suddenly thought, "God! What have I done? He's lied to me and he knows it, and he knows I know it, and here I've gone ahead and confirmed him in his lie. How big a fool can you be?" I've never seen him since, or even tried to.

It's awfully easy to moralize about things like this, and get stuffy and say that quitters come to a bad end, and so on. But that isn't the way life works a lot of the time. From reading class notes in our alumni magazine I know this man, financially, at least, is much more successful now than I am.

I'm sure one reason this incident has stuck in my mind for all these years is that I've often been tempted to quit myself when I've been on the hot seat, but, thank God, I don't think I have—not yet, anyway; I can't deny the possibility's always there. I suppose knowing that it's there helps you keep some humility, and probably also helps you keep from quitting.

"Quitting," as the word has been used here, is not a desirable solution to an emotional crisis. It is not easy to explain why without sounding somewhat pompous and pietistic. Nevertheless, some attempt at explanation has to be made. "Quitting" is an avoidance of emotional crisis essentially for the sake of *self-preservation*, regardless of the welfare of anyone else. The consequences of "quitting," for the individual and for his family and friends, are not too predictable in isolated instances, as is shown in the example just given. It is entirely conceivable that having "quit" in a crisis a person may see the fallacy in what he did and decide not to do it again. There are obvious dangers in adopting "quitting" as a way of life. It may give one the idea that this is a means of comfortably and also properly avoiding all emotional crises. This in itself is not true, and such an attitude carries the possibility not only of weakening one's own character but of hurting family, friends, and even others who are simply observers but whose code of behavior may be influenced by the example we set. Certainly "quitting" was not part of the teaching of Christ, or of any form of religion with which the author is even remotely acquainted.

There is a crucial difference between "quitting" in a crisis, as we have defined it, and seeking help in a crisis. Seeking help, whether it be from family, friends, or a professional, may often be an indication of realism, courage, and hope, rather than the opposite.

3. ABANDONMENT OF SELF–CONTROL AND RESPONSIBILITY, WITH UNRESTRAINED, RECKLESS AND IMPULSIVE BEHAVIOR

When examined closely, reckless, impulsive behavior usually turns out to be an expression of despair or a call for help, or both. If this is recognized in time, it may be possible to give the person the assistance he needs. Unfortunately, what often happens instead is that other people reject this person because they find his behavior so unacceptable; their immediate reaction is "I would never do anything like that." This is a very understandable and human reaction, but it is not helpful, because there is a fallacy in it (about which we will have more to say below), and because the troubled person becomes alienated by continual rejection, to the point where he may ultimately destroy himself.

An outstanding illustration of this is John O'Hara's *Appointment in Samarra*.[6] Although it is a novel, it could well have taken place in actual life; such things do happen, and all too often. This particular tragedy has its roots in this very assumption: "I would never do anything like that."

Julian English is a relatively young man, who is successful in business and has a nice wife, but still is a little bitter and not entirely happy. This is partly due to frustrations with his own family in earlier years, comparable to those that many people experience, which have had some influence on his life and career. At a country club party he finds himself across the table from a man with whom he has an important business association, but a bore whom Julian despises. Julian reflects, as he has done on other occasions, about how he would love to throw his drink in that man's face, and about the consternation it would cause. But he knows, of course, that he would never do such a thing. And suddenly, in the next moment, he has done it.

This sets into motion a chain of destructive events that seem to proceed inexorably. He tries to seek out the other man the next day to apologize to him, but the man refuses to see him. Especially upsetting to him is his realization, now that he is in trouble, that all the people whom he had thought of as his friends have ac-

---

[6] John O'Hara, *Appointment in Samarra* (New York: Random House, 1934).

tually resented him for years and now make use of this opportunity to deride and hurt him. Stung by this, he loses his head completely and is baited into a deplorable fight with one of these "fair weather" friends, a one-armed war veteran who actually starts the fight, although it is brought off as if Julian were the instigator.

Julian's reputation in the community is now ruined. Meanwhile his wife is shocked, confused, and angry; they quarrel, and she goes back to her parents, talking about divorce. Thus, only forty-eight hours after his original impulsive slip, he is totally alienated and alone, and his life appears to be wrecked beyond repair. Nothing goes right. While drinking by himself he even accidentally breaks one of his old all-time favorite phonograph records. So, having gotten very drunk, he commits suicide by sitting in his car with the garage door closed and the engine running.

There is a final note of sorrow in that the position of his dead body suggests that he might have changed his mind just before losing consciousness and tried to get out of the car, but did not have the strength to do so. And perhaps the worst thing of all about the tragedy is that none of the others seem to learn anything from it.

Julian English's impulsive abandonment of responsibility and self-control results in an unnecessary catastrophe that serves no useful purpose. But the story points up two important and very common fallacies. The first we have already mentioned: *"I would never do anything like that."* It may take several years after hearing about a calamity like Julian English's, whether in fiction or fact, for the truth gradually to dawn upon us that what he did we also could do. We have the same capacity for impulsiveness, bad judgment, and desperation that he had. Whether or not we are stimulated to act in that way is sometimes a matter of chance and luck. While the recognition of this may be disturbing, it can also be paradoxically reassuring, because knowing that all human beings have the potential for this kind of behavior in a crisis may help to prepare us to prevent it when we ourselves are under pressure.

The second fallacy is closely related to the first. It is the assumption that there is such a thing as a completely hopeless situation in life. There is not. Julian English apparently realized this just before he was overcome by carbon monoxide and tried to get out of his car, but he was then too weak to do it. Possibly there is an example for us, and even a very faint note of hope, in the suggestion that he may at least have made the effort.

No matter how bad the circumstances are, there is always something constructive that can be done, whether or not we realize it at the time, if we maintain our responsibility and do not throw it away recklessly. But it is only through faith that one learns this is so, and frequently it is faith in the midst of deep doubt, when self-sufficiency is plainly perceived to be a myth.

4. RESIGNATION TO A LIFE OF PERPETUAL STRUGGLE TO ENDURE CEASELESS AGONY

When immediate and almost miraculous solutions to an emotional crisis are not forthcoming, many people fear that this is what they are going to have to face for the rest of their lives. But it is not so. Some measure of personal suffering in an emotional crisis is of course inevitable, and frankly at times it may be quite severe. But to assume that such intense discomfort must be allowed to go on permanently is a wholly unacceptable idea. It is entirely contrary to biblical teaching, and furthermore it would be realistically intolerable for anyone.

5. SUICIDE

This is a subject of special importance for a variety of reasons.

We are not including here a discussion of clearly altruistic suicide, as in the actual instance of the soldier in World War I who, when a grenade about to be thrown by a comrade slipped from his hand and fell into their trench, saw the danger at once, threw himself on the grenade, and in the next instant was blown to bits, but all of the others in the trench were uninjured.

We are considering rather the plight of the person in an emotional crisis who sees no way out of his predicament, for himself and perhaps for others as well, as long as he goes on living. Would it not be simpler for all concerned if he were to do away with himself? He would presumably be at rest, and the others involved with him would be freed from the problems that seem to be created by the mere fact of his existence. The thought of suicide in such a crisis can be extremely tempting; this feeling was caught in the motion picture M*A*S*H* (1970) in a song, "Suicide Is Painless," which had almost the quality of a siren's song, luring the listener closer and closer. The expression of suicidal thoughts has been correctly interpreted as a cry for help. Unfortunately, the well-intended efforts of friends to reassure and encourage the troubled person are frequently not helpful.

A man recovering from a depression said, "People tried their best to help me when I felt bad, but it was all the same old stuff: 'Look at what a success you've been in your job. Think of your wonderful wife and children.'" He smiled. "You know that when you're really depressed, discouraged and low down, none of that means a thing to you. Your only thought about your wife and children is that they'd be better off without you."

The individual committed to a religious faith has a particular problem here, which we have touched on before: Many people assume that faith and doubt are incompatible with one another, and that therefore a truly religious person is not supposed to have doubts. Actually he may often have as many as anyone else, and perhaps even more, because he is sensitive to the injustices of the world and the responsibility that his religion requires of him seems at times staggering. On top of that, when he is not permitted by his acquaintances to have doubts, he may feel very much alone and the burden may become overpowering.

A clergyman who for years had given outstanding pastoral service to his community committed suicide. Among his survivors was a close friend who had served his own pastoral community equally well, particularly the underprivileged, and was widely known and highly regarded. This man was asked in a quiet moment of intimacy by a good friend and member of his congregation the common question, "How could someone like X possibly kill himself when he had such tremendous faith?" He answered gently, "Well, you know we clergymen are human too." Apparently, the subject was not pursued further. Before the year was up the second pastor also committed suicide.

Incidents of this kind are a constant warning to us of the danger in our being judgmental. They are profoundly depressing. But it is conceivable that they may also stimulate us, not only to think but also to seek some way or ways of action which might eventually have some constructive value. For instance, I believe that suicide, in the sense in which we have been using the word here, is in itself no solution to any problem, because further action by the individual becomes impossible, and because God has promised us that there is always another attainable solution that is better. However, one has to be extremely careful about what one says here, and how one says it. The discouraged, hopeless person who thinks of himself as unproductive may believe that ending his life would be the most altruistic thing he could do.

Suicide is not in itself a coward's way out. It is well known to all of us that brave, intelligent, perceptive people, some of whom have had religious commitments and followed them admirably, have come to a point where they have taken their own lives because they could not honestly see anything better to do for themselves and for others. While we may disagree with their decision, we must acknowledge their courageous attempts to face up to the issue. One appropriate response to these might be an effort to develop gradually a more adequate theology of emotional crisis which would hopefully help to prevent similar tragedies in the future.

In this connection, it is not at all inconsistent or two-faced for a counselor to encourage a depressed and discouraged person to try to go on living in a positive way, although he himself may be simultaneously having doubts about the purpose of continuing his own existence. One by-product of helping others may be that we sometimes find additional faith and strength for ourselves.[7]

---

[7] There is another kind of attempt to solve the problem of emotional crisis, which deserves special mention because it claims at least to have an affinity with God's good news. That is the use of the so-called "mind-expanding" drugs such as LSD, about which widely conflicting opinions have been expressed. Physicians in general are inclined to react in horror about the dangers of using these drugs. A number of other observers have commented on the fact that people who have had no previous formal or personal commitment to religion have reported their experiences with these drugs in religious terms. These professional commentators think it is conceivable that such drugs may afford one way to a genuinely religious experience. Walter Houston Clark, Emeritus Professor of Psychology and Religion at the Andover-Newton Theological School, and Walter Pahnke, a psychiatrist who has done research in this area, are among those who think that this may be so. This author has taken none of these drugs himself and has had relatively little contact with those who have. He did participate in a panel discussion that included one individual who had experimented with these drugs and ultimately discontinued them because he felt that their use led to withdrawal from the world rather than participation in it. This is also the author's impression, though it is admittedly gained from second-hand information. Further investigation will be necessary before any authoritative opinion can be offered.

CHAPTER 4
CONSTRUCTIVE WAYS OF DEALING WITH EMOTIONAL CRISIS

To these five kinds of unsuccessful efforts to resolve an emotional crisis, there is an alternative. In contrast to the others it is not only workable but also consistent with God's good news. Its directives can be found in the Bible. Since this alternative is based on faith and trust in God, it is naturally important to understand as much as we can about what faith and trust in God really mean. In attempting to make any statement about the nature of this kind of faith and trust, someone without formal theological training is obviously skating on very thin ice. Nevertheless, the author feels that from independent study and from personal and professional experience, including contacts with the clergy, he has learned several facts about faith and trust which were much less clear to him beforehand, and which he has since found are also unclear to a number of people who come to him for help. These are:

1. Faith and trust are not *irrational*, but arational. That is, they are not governed primarily by the intellect. Here we are reminded of the comment of Ecclesiastes quoted above, that being "over-wise" can be self-destructive.

2. Fundamentally, faith and trust are not more or

less permanent states of feeling good or feeling confident. This is an extremely common misconception. Faith and trust are rather what keep us going even though we may not be conscious of having any faith or trust left.

3. Faith, trust, and enlightenment must all be sought in the finite, rather than by cutting oneself off totally from the world in the hope of finding something transcendental: This opinion is shared by more than one religious tradition:

a. It is recorded in the Gospels that to the self-righteous Pharisees who were asking for a sign as a proof of Jesus' exalted position, Jesus replied, "Why doth this generation seek after a sign? Verily I say unto you, there shall be no sign given unto this generation (Mark 8:12, KJV)."

b. Masters of Zen Buddhism have given this sort of response to their eager pupils for centuries. For example, one pupil asked his master what the essence of Zen is. The master replied, "Do you hear the murmuring stream?" The pupil said, "Yes, master." The master then told him, "If so, here is the entrance." [1]

In other words, nothing is hidden. Our solutions are available in the world around us and if we seek them there, we will eventually find them.

4. Faith, trust, and enlightenment, although fundamentally religious matters, are often less romantic and supersensual than the language of the New Testament may perhaps suggest. This may confuse the troubled person who expects to be saved by some sort

---

[1] D. T. Suzuki, *Zen Buddhism* (Anchor Book; New York: Doubleday, 1956), p. 153.

of miracle and thereby fails to see the real way in which his crisis can be resolved.

For example, a perfectionistic student had trouble writing papers for his courses because he could not express himself in ways that satisfied him and that he assumed were necessary in order to impress his teachers with his ability. Consequently he got further and further behind in his work. Eventually he sought help from a counselor. On one visit he reported that he was having such difficulty writing a paper that he had spent most of the previous evening composing a prayer to God asking divine aid in clarifying the cause of his problem and assisting him in handling it. He brought the prayer with him to the counselor and read it. The counselor pointed out to him that we are told in the New Testament that God knows what our needs are, and asked him whether, instead of composing such a lengthy prayer, he would not have done better to spend the time on the paper that was due, even if he were not entirely satisfied with what he had written.

We are now ready to turn to the Bible to see what directives it has for us when we are in emotional crisis, and how we can make use of them. *The biblical passages which follow are those which contain significant directives. A trained theologian would undoubtedly add to and improve upon these choices and interpretations. These directives are not in themselves magical or immediate solutions to crisis. Rather they are guidelines to constructive and positive courses of action, which will vary somewhat depending on the individual situation. There is no single specific course of action that is necessarily appropriate for everyone in all situations.*

Particularly characteristic of these directives is that

each one contains, whether explicitly or implicitly, both a divine promise and a divine demand. This is as it should be. Robert Bonthius has stated that a problem cannot be dealt with biblically unless the matter of divine demand is included.

> I. "COME UNTO ME, ALL YE THAT LABOR AND ARE HEAVY LADEN, AND I WILL GIVE YOU REST. TAKE MY YOKE UPON YOU, AND LEARN OF ME; FOR I AM MEEK AND LOWLY IN HEART; AND YE SHALL FIND REST UNTO YOUR SOULS. FOR MY YOKE IS EASY, AND MY BURDEN IS LIGHT (MATT. 11:28–30, KJV)."

This is an especially beautiful and appealing part of the Gospels. Only God or, in this instance, the Son of God, can make a promise as sweeping as this that we can accept as true. But it is true. Through faith it gradually becomes possible to understand that even in an unfair world *"I will give you rest."*

We are not told how soon rest will come, or in what form and for whom, or even how long it will last; but the implication is plain that it will be comforting and satisfying, and not so long delayed as to be purposeless when it comes.

We should note that the reassurance in "I will give you rest" is preceded by a demand, although a very gentle and quiet one: *"Come unto me."* There is no suggestion of insistence or forcing in this demand. It is more like an invitation that one is free either to accept or to decline. Nonetheless, the message seems unmistakable that in order to receive God's promised rest we will first need to turn or "come" to him in some way. A number of people in turmoil may frequently "come to" God without realizing at first that this is actually what they are doing.

We should also note that "I will give you rest" is linked, however gently, with another demand: "Take my yoke upon you, and learn of me." This latter demand is immediately softened by another promise: ". . . for I am meek and lowly in heart; and ye shall find rest unto your souls. For my yoke is easy, and my burden is light."

"Come unto me," "learn of me," and even "take my yoke upon you" are not to be misconstrued as advice to rush out and join a church at once in the expectation that this in itself is going to cause or even facilitate the happening of some personal good. To do this would be to miss completely the purpose of religion and of the church. Church membership has essentially nothing to do with the relief or persistence of emotional distress. The author perceives these three directives as meaning rather: "Trust me. Listen to what I am going to tell you now. Pay attention."

"My yoke is easy, and my burden is light" is an assurance that nothing is expected of us that is impossible for us to do. Again, this is such a definite statement, and of such immensity, that only God is capable of assuring us that it is true. It often takes some time to recognize how true it is. Therefore, if what we are trying to do appears *realistically* impossible, we may do well to consider whether we may be trying to do it in the wrong way (for example, being too perfectionistic in attempting to carry out our plans and hopes, which is a common weakness in most of us), or whether perhaps we should not be trying to do this particular thing at all, but something else for which we may have really more interest, aptitude, and natural enthusiasm.

II. "THIS IS THE DAY WHICH THE LORD HATH MADE; WE WILL REJOICE AND BE GLAD IN IT (PS. 118:24, KJV)."

Here we have chosen to go back to the Old Testament because, although it takes us out of chronological order, the directives in this passage seem to follow rather naturally the ones given in the passage from Matthew. They are some of the consequences of taking God's yoke upon us.

Again, there is a divine promise and a divine demand. The *promise* is that this is not just a day, but "the day which the Lord hath made." In other words, every day contains the possibility of something special—an opportunity, however slight, for some sort of unique and meaningful decision or action, whether one recognizes it or not. Obviously some days contain more possibilities and opportunities than others, but there is a distinct implication that there is no day without at least some trace of this.

The *demand* is contained in the words "We will rejoice and be glad in it." Out of gratitude to God for the day, this is what we are to do. But an obvious question arises immediately: Does this mean literally that we are to sing and shout for joy, even on bad days? The author does not believe so. For example, how could Viktor Frankl possibly have behaved in this fashion while confined to the horrors of a German concentration camp? The fact is that some of our days are truly bad and even miserable. To claim otherwise would represent an unrealistic denial, a hollow pretense, which would eventually break down because this kind of self-deception is impossible. This would contradict the New Testament assurance that in a crisis God expects nothing from us which we cannot do.

Since joy may include sorrow, "rejoicing" is not a single standard and uniform procedure fitting all occasions. It seems more likely that there is a kind of spectrum of rejoicing in which there are various degrees, the simplest probably being a willingness to accept the day as it is and see what one can do with it. One's response to this Old Testament directive then might be somewhat as follows: "Frankly, I don't see one good thing about this day. I'm tired and discouraged, and I certainly don't feel like rejoicing about this day at all. But as long as I don't have to do that, I guess I can just go out and meet it and see what happens." This in itself may be one genuine form of rejoicing. It may be all that God expects at that time. On certain days rejoicing realistically may consist of nothing more than simply getting through the day. There are periods when the seemingly overworked cliché of "living a day at a time" is helpful, because it enables a person to stay in motion until a purposeful direction ultimately unfolds, whereas looking too far into the future when one is discouraged may give a distorted and unduly gloomy perspective.[2]

1. A depressed man said, "The time I feel worst is

---

[2] As mentioned above, if most or all days are really as bad as this, some change of personal direction may be indicated, since it is not God's intention for us to live in perpetual wretchedness.

when the alarm goes off in the morning and I wake up and the whole situation hits me right in the face. All I want to do is roll over and pull the covers over my head. But then in a little while I hear the children moving around, and that gets me up because I know I ought to be there and have breakfast with them. By the time I start to shave my wife is up, and as long as the others are up I make it somehow, and once I'm out of the house on my way to work the day seems to take care of itself.

"There are occasional mornings when my wife and children have to get an early start, which leaves me alone in the house. One such morning I felt so rotten that after breakfast I got back into bed. Presently I looked at the clock and knew that if I was going to get to work on time I ought to be up and in the shower right then. But every fiber in my body said, 'No. I just can't do it.' So I lay there quietly, and every few minutes I'd look at the clock, and of course it got a little later, and a little later, but everything in me still said 'No.' Finally I looked at the clock and thought, 'If I get up now and move fast and get out of here I'll still be half an hour late to work.' That got me up, even though I still didn't want to get up. I'm sure I knew all along that somehow I was going to get up, but that I was going to wait until it was 'now or never,' and that would give me the little extra push I needed to do it.

"I'm quite aware that there could come a morning when I might not get up. But, strangely enough, I think knowing that helps me get up. I want to put as much time as possible between me and the morning I might not get up, until some day when I feel good enough to be pretty sure that that morning isn't going to come after all. Then I'll really be able to rejoice in the day. But right now just getting going is the best I can do."

2. A young married woman who had been depressed for several weeks telephoned her counselor the day before her next appointment, saying, "I feel at the end of my rope and I don't know how I can possibly last through the day. I'm putting myself in your hands, even if it means I have to go to the hospital." The counselor asked her, "What have you been doing today?" He was rather expecting that she might say she had done little or nothing because she was feeling so badly. However, somewhat to his surprise, she enumerated a list of household chores that was quite impressive, especially since the day was only half over. He told her, "It sounds to me as though you've done a good deal. I know how you feel; but I think you're actually getting through the day very well. If you just keep on doing what needs to be done around the home one thing at a time, until your husband gets home, and don't fight the depression, you'll make it through the day all right. I wouldn't tell you that if I didn't believe it. And I'll see you tomorrow at our usual time." She got through the day with less discomfort than she had expected. It was not too long before her depression went away.

One of this woman's problems was that she was like those people whom we have previously described as suffering from the misconception that to have fears and doubts is a sign of a "bad Christian." Understanding that this is not so seemed to be one thing that helped her handle difficult days much more easily.

Some support for this idea that there are different degrees of rejoicing is found in the English hymn "Lord of the Dance." The hymn has caught an essential element of Christianity—a rather quiet optimism that bubbles on unchecked in spite of calamities which are fully recognized and appreciated. It has a combination of a light, happy touch and a curious dignity, which make singing it in a group a strangely moving experience. The hymn follows:

> "I danced in the morning when the world was begun,[3]
> And I danced in the moon and the stars and the sun,
> And I came down from heaven and I danced on the earth;
> At Bethlehem I had my birth.
>
> (*Refrain*) "Dance, then, wherever you may be,
> I am the Lord of the Dance, said He,
> And I'll lead you all, wherever you may be,
> And I'll lead you all in the dance, said He.
>
> "I danced for the scribe and the Pharisee,
> But they would not dance and they wouldn't follow me;
> I danced for the fishermen, for James and John,
> They came with me and the dance went on. (*Refrain*)

---

[3] Sydney Carter, "Lord of the Dance." Copyright 1963 by Galliard Ltd. All rights reserved. Used by permission of Galaxy Music Corp., N.Y., sole U.S. agent.

"I danced on the Sabbath and I cured the lame;
 The holy people said it was a shame;
 They whipped and they stripped and they hung me high,
 And they left me there on a cross to die. (*Refrain*)

"I danced on a Friday when the sky turned black;
 It's hard to dance with the devil on your back;
 They buried my body and they thought I'd gone,
 But I am the Dance and I still go on. (*Refrain*)

"They cut me down and I leap up high;
 I am the Life that'll never, never die;
 I'll live in you if you'll live in me;
 I am the Lord of the Dance, said He." (*Refrain*)

Attention is called particularly to the second line of the fourth verse: "It's hard to dance with the devil on your back." This is probably one of the greatest understatements in history. It has meaning for us because it is such a vivid description of how many people in an emotional crisis feel—that is, almost flattened by a weight so oppressive that it seems unbearable. To dance, or "to rejoice" in the sense that most of us ordinarily use this word, is not only hard under such conditions; it is impossible. Christ did not literally dance on the cross! He did not literally dance, for that matter, in any of the other situations in his life on earth recorded in the Bible. The message of this hymn is one of joy, which the writer of the hymn has chosen to exemplify by the concept of the dance. But how one is able to carry out the message of rejoicing is bound to vary considerably depending on the circumstances in which he happens to be at any given time.

III. "ARISE, TAKE UP THY BED, AND WALK (MATT. 9:2–8, KJV)." [4]

At first glance this appears to be purely a demand, but there is also a promise plainly implied in it, which is that through faith (that is, the willingness to make the effort) and God's love for us the person will be able to carry out the demand—in this case, to "arise and walk." "Arising and walking," like "rejoicing," may take a variety of forms. Which form is chosen as the most appropriate will be determined by the individual situation. It may consist of:

1. Doing what needs to be done at a particular time. A pastor had been coming for help because of a persistent depression. He too was under the impression that his being depressed made him a "bad Christian" and a hypocrite in trying to give assistance and comfort to others when he himself had doubts. At one time he was especially bothered by the prospect of calling on a parishioner whose husband had just died. He commented in distress, "I don't know what to say to her. I can't think of any good I can be to her when I feel so bad myself, so I keep putting off going to see her, but I know that's wrong, too. I don't know what to do. I simply can't think of what to say to her."

The counselor told him, "That's right. Of course you don't know what to say to her, because you haven't seen her and you have no way of knowing how she's taking her husband's death. Wouldn't the best thing be for you to go ahead and call on her anyway? When

---

[4] This statement by Jesus appears in all the Gospels, although with some minor variations in the wording (also Mark 2:3–12; Luke 5:18–25; John 5:2–9), but the essence of the message is the same in each.

you see how she is, and listen to what she tells you, you'll have a lot better idea of what to do for her. Besides, you don't have to say too much. There isn't a great deal anybody can say at a time like that. I think what will mean the most to her won't be what you said as much as the fact that you came." The pastor accepted this suggestion, and not long afterward his depression began improving.

2. *Doing what might be done as an arbitrary choice among several alternatives.* An anxious and depressed man who had been seeing a counselor for some weeks telephoned him one afternoon to report that he was feeling so discouraged that he had not been to work that day but had stayed in bed and was wondering whether there was any point in living any longer and whether he would not do better to commit suicide. Something in the way in which this was expressed convinced the counselor that this was a call for help rather than an expression of serious suicidal intent. He said to the man, "Let me tell you what to do that will help you. First, get up. I know you can do that. Lying in bed in the daytime just makes you worry more about yourself. Then find something or some things around the house that need doing, and do them. It doesn't matter what they are as long as you're doing something. That will divert you somewhat. It won't be magic, but it will help. Also, don't shut yourself off from your family; talk to them and stay with them."

The man got up. As he looked around the home he gradually noticed a number of things that needed to be done. He decided to start by repairing one of his child's toys. Next he thought he would clean up the garage a bit. By the end of the afternoon he had completed several odd jobs of this sort and was feeling somewhat better. That particular experience seemed to be a crucial one for him, because from then on he improved progressively and two or three months later felt well enough so that counseling was terminated by mutual consent.

3. *Temporary withdrawal from the conflict and engaging in something else, such as recreation, in order to allow a fresh perspective to develop.* At times this may be a perfectly sensible thing to do.

A first year law student came for help in the latter part of the school year because of depression, anxiety, and irritability. His problem was a common one. He had greatly enjoyed college but had no idea of what he wanted to do after graduation. He had finally decided to enter law school. For a number of months he had tried to deny that he had mixed feelings about doing this. But his classmates in law school were now very interested in their work and felt a sense of purpose in it for themselves which he did not feel at all. The tedium and frustration he had met with in law school had been a shattering contrast to his college experience. But he was bewildered because he did not feel drawn to any other line of work he could think of either. He thought it best that he finish what remained of the first law school year, but after that he did not know where to turn. His family told him that he was simply lazy. He could not be sure that they were wrong, but still he could not quite believe that they were right. Originally he had planned a summer vacation trip to Europe with a friend, but he was now in such a state of inner turmoil that he was afraid of having an emotional breakdown if he went that far away from home.

After some discussion with the counselor, however, they both concluded that the European trip might be just what he needed during the summer, because he could have a good time with a friend for two months and gradually forget about the struggle. Then, having allowed the dust to settle, he would probably be better able at the end of the summer to decide what to do next. In the fall he reported that the European vacation had been a tremendous success, and that he had subsequently resolved to give law school a good try for one more year and, if his feelings about it had not changed, he would find something else to do and have no regrets. It turned out that the last two years of law school were far more satisfying to him than the first one, and he went on to graduate.

4. The decision either to move in a new direction or to stay in the same one but with a different motivation than before. Such a decision often is not easy because one's motives are apt to be suspect, not only to others but also to oneself. Yet the decision must be made. Until it is made, one knows no peace.

A thirty-two-year-old unmarried physician announced after completing his tour of duty in the Armed Forces that he was leaving medicine to go to graduate school and study the decorative arts. He said, "Actually, I've had this vocational crisis going on for nearly ten years. It nearly threw me seven or eight years ago and I had to get some help. After that I thought I'd resolved it, but I never really did; I see now I'd just put it off, and it got much less acute. I stayed in medicine but I never really knew where I was going in it, and I knew some day I'd have to figure that one out. I couldn't see myself as either a practitioner or a researcher.

"While I was in the service I went to Rome and saw the Vatican Museum and the Sistine Chapel. They really rocked me. I realized that nothing in medicine had ever interested me the way those things did. There was no mistaking the fact that it was time for me to change. What I'm aiming for now is eventually to be a curator of painting in a museum. A lot of my relatives and friends aren't going to understand why I'm moving out of an established field like medicine after having spent so much time in it; but it makes sense to me. I'm still young enough so that it isn't too late for me to do it, and I know I'll never have a chance like this again."

A young married man came for help with a marital problem. He was beginning to realize what mixed feelings he had toward his wife, and how competitive he felt toward her so that he had failed to perceive and meet her needs as a woman. In spite of all this, he said on several different occasions, "I know we've got troubles, but I hope we can straighten them out. I like her. I don't really want a divorce." The counselor told him, "My primary purpose in trying to help you isn't necessarily to break up your marriage. If there's something good in the marriage, then counseling should strengthen it rather than the reverse." This indeed was what seemed to happen in the counseling process.

Interestingly enough, an acquaintance of this man was also undertaking marital counseling at the same time with a different counselor, but he had already left his wife, and his life at the moment was quite chaotic. He said to the first man, "Your counselor apparently believes in adjustment. Mine believes in progress." Certainly what constitutes progress is often debatable, but it is risky to assume that change per se is synonymous with progress.

5. *Naturally, those who are ill in bed will not be able to "arise and walk" in the literal sense.* For some of these it may mean making the best use of what time they have left on earth. There is Viktor Frankl's moving account of "a young woman who had led an utterly pampered existence" and who "was one day unexpectedly thrown into a concentration camp."

> There she fell ill and was visibly wasting away. A few days before she died she said these very words: "Actually I am grateful to my fate for having treated me so harshly. In my former middle-class existence I certainly had things a great deal too easy. . . ." She saw death coming and looked it squarely in the eye. From her bed in the infirmary she could catch a glimpse of a chestnut tree in blossom outside the window. She spoke of this tree often, though from where the sick woman's head lay just one twig with two blossoms was visible. "This tree is my only friend in solitude," the woman said. "I converse with it." Was this a hallucination? . . . Did she think the tree was "answering" her? What strange dialogue was this; what had the flowering tree "said" to the dying woman? "It says: 'I am here, I am here—I am life, eternal life.' " [5]

There are others who in the course of a grave and lingering illness may have not only a new and unex-

---

[5] Viktor Frankl, *The Doctor and the Soul* (New York: Alfred A. Knopf, 1957), p. 132. Copyright 1955, © 1965 Alfred A. Knopf, Inc.

pected view of the wonders of life, as this woman did, but also an eventual opportunity to "arise and walk" literally, when they have recovered from their physical disabilities, and put these fresh insights into some form of action. But once they are well again, the vision may fade rapidly and perhaps never be recovered. One man at a party said, reminded by something, "When I was seriously ill and lay in bed looking at the world outside my window, I saw an overpowering beauty that I'd never before known was there. I was sure then that if I ever got well my life would never be the same as before. I'd remember this always and do something special with it." He smiled ruefully and, as he turned to go to the bar, added, "Then I got well and I forgot about it."

To "arise and walk" involves making a decision to do the best one can under the circumstances.

The promise is that God will recognize what we are doing and respond in a way that we can perceive. The man who in Jesus' parable hid his one talent in the earth aimed too low and was too interested in protecting himself, so that he had to suffer the consequences (Matt. 25:14–30).

IV. "AND THEY BROUGHT TO HIM A MAN WHO WAS DEAF AND HAD AN IMPEDIMENT IN HIS SPEECH; . . . AND LOOKING UP TO HEAVEN [JESUS] SAID TO HIM, . . . 'BE OPENED.' AND HIS EARS WERE OPENED, HIS TONGUE WAS RELEASED, AND HE SPOKE PLAINLY (MARK 7:32, 34–35, RSV)."

This quotation is from the account of Jesus healing

the deaf mute. Here, too, is a promise and a demand, but they are of a somewhat different nature from those that we have discussed before. For one thing, both promise and demand are contained in the same two words, *"Be opened."* The promise is obvious: something shall be done to help the person; he shall be opened. But the brevity and terseness of Jesus' statement seem to imply that more than just a promise is intended here. He does not say, for instance, "Fear not, you shall be opened," or even simply, "You shall be opened," or "You are being opened." The words come out more abruptly—"Be opened"—almost like a command, which in this case is obviously addressed to the deaf mute and to nobody else.

There is a suggestion that in order to "be opened" something, however slight, is demanded of the sufferer—perhaps a grain of faith, perhaps a willingness to respond in some way to God or to man. It seems reasonable to assume that, compared to what God can and will do for him in the situation, what is required of the sufferer himself in order to "be opened" must be relatively small, perhaps even minute, although to him it may appear as if it were disconcertingly large. But the deaf mute plainly was incapable of conquering his disability, or even the major part of it, by his own efforts. Jesus did not say to him "Open yourself," but "Be opened." God will do the opening—that is the promise. Man must be willing to be opened—that is the demand. In other words, he must be receptive to an understanding of what God's will is for him in the situation and act on it as soon as he knows what it is.

To those of us who are either in emotional crisis ourselves or trying to help other people out of it, this message, "Be opened," is of very special significance. In attempting to follow the three biblical directives we have previously been discussing, we must admit that we have been to some extent groping in the dark in search of God's promised rest, endeavoring to maintain our faith in spite of serious doubt and with no magical sign to reassure us; keeping somehow in motion, trying to use our best judgment in making necessary decisions, but never being sure whether we were going in the right or wrong direction. Now we begin to see that this groping in the midst of uncertainty has a purpose to it, because it keeps us in touch with the finite where we have been told enlightenment is to be found. It keeps us from turning completely inward upon ourselves and helps us turn outward toward the world around us and the people in it, be it ever so slightly. It helps us avoid total self-absorption in which we cannot be aware of God's message. The eventual result of following these directives as best we can is that we shall "be opened." Incidentally, it is apparent that the biblical directives quoted in this work overlap somewhat with one another. For example, it will be clear that Viktor Frankl's dying woman mentioned above under the heading "Arise, take up thy bed and walk" (though she could do so only in a very figurative sense) was also "opened" to a dimension of life the existence of which she had never even dreamed of before.

To "be opened" in the course of an emotional crisis may have a number of meanings, any or all of which may apply, depending on the particular case. It may mean an understanding of the true cause of the crisis and what the person or persons involved need to do to resolve it. A number of people, though not all, have at least some comprehension of the nature and cause of the emotional crises facing them, but are in anguish, largely because they are confused as to how to handle themselves and what specific steps to take. "Being opened," among other things, clarifies the advisable course of action.

"Being opened" may in some instances take place suddenly. The Zen Buddhists, for example, think of profound enlightenment essentially as a sudden process. One of their favorite descriptions of such enlightenment is "The bottom of the pail has broken through!" [6] With the majority of people in emotional turmoil, however, "being opened" seems to take place more gradually.

One instance of gradually "being opened" had to do with a man who, after having seen a counselor for several weeks because of anxiety and depression, said to him one day, "You know, it's a funny thing. I feel just as bad as I did before, but somehow it doesn't bother me as much. Is that possible?" This struck the counselor as the beginning of the man's "being opened." He replied, "Yes, it certainly is possible. I think it's an important step. You're starting to be less concerned about how you feel and more concerned about what's going on around you. As this keeps up the next thing that will probably happen is that you'll feel less bad less often." This is what did happen.

But "being opened," as has been said already, is not confined simply to the solution of difficulties in one's

---

[6] *In Quest of Wholeness: Dialogues with Thomas Hora* (mimeographed compilation of Hora's papers and group discussions, by graduate students at the American Foundation of Religion and Psychiatry, New York City), p. 80.

worldly life, so that one can go on again just as he has before. The surpassing of such obstacles may lead to a still further "opening" much greater than one had expected. This aspect of "being opened" is very hard to put into words, but we must nevertheless try. It may take time for it to develop, but after experiencing it an individual is never quite the same as he had previously been. He has a new view of the world, a new appreciation of it, a new sense of purpose and dedication, but also a feeling of humility because he realizes that man is not fundamentally the master of things. There begins to stir within him a feeling of reverence toward the true Master. One might say that it is as though a prayer had been unexpectedly answered.

In fact, the subject of prayer is very relevant to the whole problem of emotional crisis. One of the times, though by no means the only time, we are encouraged to pray is when we are in trouble and turmoil. What is not so clear is *how* we should pray at such a time. People are baffled by their observation that some prayers are apparently not answered, and they wonder why this should be so, if prayer is as important in religion as the church declares it to be. Is there such a thing as unanswered prayer, and if so, why?

Perhaps we may not be able to answer these questions. But if we are to make any attempt to do so, it would seem logical for us to start by considering Christ's prayer in the Garden of Gethsemane. He had taken Peter, James, and John, three of his most loyal disciples, and instructed them to stay with him and watch. It is recorded that he said repeatedly: "Father, take away this cup from me; *nevertheless not what I will, but what thou willst*" (italics added; see Matthew 26:41–45; Mark 14:35–41; Luke 22:40–46). Many commentators have emphasized the fact that this latter statement of Christ's (that is, "according to *Thy* will, not mine") is one of the most essential aspects of any prayer, and also one of the easiest to forget. God, of course, did not intervene to prevent the crucifixion, and Christ submitted to it. It might be argued, therefore, that this is an instance of unanswered prayer, were it not for the qualifying "not according to my will, but Thine." The New Testament tells us that God did answer Christ's prayer, but it was through the resurrection that he answered it.

It is also worth noting that the three disciples slept while Christ was praying, so that they did not watch with him as he had asked them to do. Moreover, when Christ was apprehended, all the disciples forsook him and fled (Mark 14:50), and Peter denied him three times. This illustrates the greatest and most persistent obstacle in religion: in spite of everything, man does not trust God. Two results of this are:

1. The purpose of prayer is often misunderstood, because the will of God is not considered. Prayer then becomes an attempt to manipulate God into granting our requests on our terms, without realizing that God already knows our needs (Matthew 6:31–34).

2. Man tends to desert God and Christ in times of crisis, either in the interest of self-concern and self-protection as the disciples did, or else by blaming God if his prayers are not answered in the way he expects, or if a catastrophe happens (we say, "Where was God? Why didn't he prevent this?")—in spite of God's promise not to desert us. Again it comes down to the matter of faith and trust.

It is probable that prayer is always answered by God in some way, but not necessarily in the way we assume, so that in clinging to our preconceptions we may fail to perceive God's answer.

Here it is well worth noting what Thomas Hora has to say about prayer.[7] It is interesting that in this instance we have a psychiatrist discussing prayer from a religious point of view, which Hora, having extensively studied both Eastern and Western religions, is well qualified to do. He points out that common views of prayer are mostly intermittent and sporadic modes of worshiping:

1. Ritualistic prayer is offered either to gain favor with primitive and usually wrathful gods, or as a quest for status in a community of like-minded people.

2. Intellectual prayer he describes as "a kind of mental vanity indulging itself in pretty phraseology and verbiage."

3. Emotional prayer is mostly "self-indulgent wallowing in emotion under the pretext of piety."

4. Sensuous prayer is close to the above except for the emphasis on sensory stimuli, such as flagellation or other forms of mortification of the flesh.

In contrast to these, he distinguishes what he calls *ceaseless prayer*, which is something about which we do not too often hear, although "ceaseless prayer" is actually a paraphrase of Paul, "pray without ceasing (1 Thess. 5:17, KJV)." He defines ceaseless prayer as something consistent, continuous, a way of life; not a method of trying to influence God, but to be influenced by him; not an endeavor to tell God what he

---

[7] Ibid., pp. 85–124.

should do for us, but an attempt to bring our consciousness to the point where we can understand what God has to say to us. This statement of Hora's is one way of explaining what is meant by "being opened."

Hora has some particular comments to make about intercessory prayer, prayer for the welfare of others. He says it is undeniable that intercessory prayer can be effective (he does not attempt to give any grounds, but simply makes the statement). In his opinion the effectiveness of intercessory prayer is greatly facilitated if the one who intercedes for the other is the kind of person whose way of life could be called a kind of ceaseless prayer. The term used by Hora to describe this sort of person is "a beneficial presence," that is, one whom it is a joy and comfort to be near to, regardless of how little he or she says—a person whose consciousness is, at least in some measure, in harmony with God. It may be helpful to understand that this may be more of an ideal than an actuality, especially since the one example of a "beneficial presence" specifically named by Hora is Jesus Christ. Still, knowing that we are bound to fall short of perfection should not stop us from hoping to become as "beneficial" as we can.

It is interesting and significant that elsewhere Hora has made the same statement about counseling as about prayer, namely, that it is not something one *does*, but something one *lives*.[8] One might then suspect that: (1) prayer and pastoral counseling, if accepted as parts of one continuous process or way of life, must be intimately related to one another; and

---

[8] Thomas Hora, "Tao, Zen, and Existential Psychotherapy," *Psychologia*, 2 (1959), 236.

(2) since counseling could be considered as a kind of intercession in behalf of another, pastoral counseling may be basically one form of intercessory prayer. This means that the fundamental source of understanding of pastoral counseling must be theological.

In this connection, one question that might be asked is what the function of the pastoral counselor is.[9] It is to *understand*. We are told in the New Testament that God is love. Hora has said repeatedly that love is not primarily an emotion as many people think, but a form of knowledge.[10] It is understanding another person and being understood by that person. Both are in harmony with each other and therefore in harmony with God because the love of God is inseparable from the love of one's neighbor. It is through this kind of understanding that people in emotional crisis can "be opened."

1. The pastoral counselor listens to hear what the troubled person is actually trying to tell him, and responds in a natural way.

A woman, twice married and once divorced, was referred to a counselor because of serious difficulties with the second marriage. The wife and second husband were seen separately, and it seemed evident that this marriage, too, was already beyond repair. The couple had no common interests and could not communicate with each other at all, and they knew it. The

---

[9] In this context "pastoral counselor" is any counselor who takes the religious dimension of emotional crisis seriously. Thus we could be describing a psychiatrist, psychologist, pastor, etc.

[10] *In Quest of Wholeness: Dialogues with Thomas Hora*, op. cit., pp. 132–33.

counselor therefore supported the woman in her intention to seek a divorce. Although she had decided this was best, she was greatly troubled by having had two marital failures, and kept repeating to the counselor that she did not want to go on like this for the rest of her life.

While the woman was speaking, the counselor was struck by the tone of her voice, which became progressively louder and higher-pitched, until she was almost shouting. This brought home to him the reality and intensity of her desperation, which in turn somehow gave him a feeling that he might be able to help her. He told her quietly, "Look, you don't have to shout at me like that. I understand you. I know you don't want this to happen again, and I'm going to do everything I can to help you keep it from happening." After a pause she said in much calmer tones, "I think this is what I've felt I've had to do all my life to get people to pay any attention to me—to shout at them, throw myself at them, really force myself on them—and do it right away. I've been so scared of losing people that I don't believe I've ever dared take time to think whether I honestly cared about someone or not." The counselor replied, "Well, you don't have to do that any more now." From then on rapport between her and the counselor was excellent. She went ahead with the divorce and ultimately entered into a third marriage, which proved to be a very good one.

It happened that this woman had always had strong religious interests and had done an impressive amount of study in theology entirely on her own. The referring source had made note of this, but was inclined to view it as unrealistic and an attempt to escape from the problems of actual life. However, at least during his own relationship with her, the counselor felt that her religious faith had been of real value to her.

2. The pastoral counselor is in no way an unrealistic or mystical source of communication with God. There are no dazzling visions, no brilliant colors. Rather it is as if one's vision had cleared so that for the first time he sees, among other things, his mission or part in the world as it was meant to be.

3. The pastoral counselor does not allow personal pride to carry him beyond his limits of competence. Reinhold Niebuhr's warning to all of us against pride is timely here. The counselor is human and fallible. He cannot hope to approach Christ's effectiveness as a "beneficial presence." [11]

4. Closely related to this, the pastoral counselor does not have to try to be a magician, "pulling a rabbit out of a hat," because of his own misinterpreted expectations from his professional training, or because he can tell that many troubled people who come to him are hoping or expecting that he will perform a miracle for them.

The story of the rich man in the New Testament illustrates a situation in which Jesus himself did not attempt to perform a miracle (Matt. 19:16–22; Mark 10:17–22; Luke 18:18–24). The man wanted to know how it might be possible for him to enter the kingdom of heaven, but when Jesus told him that he must first sell all he had and give it to the poor, he could not bring himself to do that. Instead, he went away

---

[11] Reinhold Niebuhr, *Beyond Tragedy* (New York: Charles Scribner's Sons, 1948).

sadly. Jesus did not run after him to persuade him to reconsider, nor did he try to convert him by a miracle.

5. Most people in emotional crisis try to help themselves in one fashion or another, but their methods are very often unsuccessful. The pastoral counselor frequently can be useful in enabling these people to see that they are trying to reach God, but in the wrong ways.

We have commented on this earlier, in discussing Hora's analogy of the man swimming with the current rather than against it, and Buber's statement concerning the man who is able to accept his fear and "relax into it." The instinctive and very natural reaction of people is to try to get rid of whatever makes them uncomfortable, including symptoms, by a direct attack—for instance, to "kill it" with an antibiotic or to "cut it out" by surgery. In an emotional crisis, where there is apt to be anxiety or depression, the reaction is usually to attempt to "push it away." But intangibles cannot be pushed away like this. Instead, one simply becomes more involved with what he would like to forget. An intelligent woman once said, "I don't know what I can do with this anxiety *except* fight with it." The counselor told her, "All that does is to keep stirring it up. If you get used to the idea of leaving it alone, it will gradually dry up like a plant that isn't watered." Like many other things in life, "leaving it alone" is much easier to talk about than to do. It often takes a little time to accustom oneself to doing this. When a person's attention is freed from the symptoms, he is ready to "be opened."

6. The pastoral counselor is not the only, or sometimes even the most important, means by which God's

word is transmitted to people in emotional crisis. Friends, family, the community, work, and other things may also be of great help.

An overly pleasant and mild-mannered man consulted a counselor because of periodic outbursts of rage, which were distressing to him and also to his family. Underneath his placid and amiable exterior he had concealed for a long time a great deal of unexpressed anger and suspicion of other people which he could no longer steadily contain. Part of his subsequent improvement appeared to stem from his recognition that the counselor did not view him with a detached cold curiosity, as he had feared, but was genuinely concerned about him and wanted to help. However, there was no question that his wife, who displayed great sensitivity and understanding and to whom he became able to talk more and more openly, had also made a very essential contribution. In trying to assess the whole situation after counseling had terminated, it was the counselor's opinion that of the two of them *the wife had been more important* in enabling her husband to "be opened" than the counselor.

7. The pastoral counselor can serve as one medium of transmitting God's truth. Hora has compared the counselor to a glass window pane, which neither actively nor passively interferes with the reception and understanding of God's truth.[12] This is not only an interesting analogy but also a useful one. The aim is

---

[12] Thomas Hora, "Existential Psychotherapy" in *Current Psychiatric Therapies*, ed. Jules H. Masserman, 2 (New York: Grune & Stratton, 1962), 31, 38–39.

appropriate, even though no counselor can hope to be as flawless as that.

Indeed, there are times when what constitutes "God's truth" in a given situation may be unclear to the counselor as well as to the person in emotional crisis. In cases of this kind the counselor must use his best judgment and hope to be a channel which God can use to communicate his Truth.[13]

A young woman who had moved away from her home town to work wrote her parents that she and a young man were living together. Her parents were extremely upset, and told her that her morals and view of life were very distorted and that she should see a pastoral counselor. She did consult a counselor, not because she felt a need to do so, but because she was truly fond of her parents and wanted to be reasonable. The counselor's impression was that she had carefully considered all the possible outcomes of this step before having taken it. She felt she truly loved the man. She was aware that there was no assurance that the relationship would endure, but she said she was prepared to face that possibility if it came about, and meanwhile was willing to take the risk.

Her parents lived in another city, and anything less than talking to them face to face he felt would be undesirable, because the chance of mutual misunderstanding would be too great. He finally said to the young woman, "It's plain that you've already made up your mind what you're going to do. I don't think

---

[13] Joseph Fletcher, *Situation Ethics* (Philadelphia: Westminster Press, 1966), p. 152.

you've made a hasty decision, but I am concerned as to what might happen if it doesn't work out as you'd hoped. I believe the best thing I can do is simply to be available to you and your parents if you should ever want me. Here's my address and phone number."

The young woman seemed in good spirits as she left. The counselor, after having let her out, thought, "That's really a tough problem. What do you do with it if you're a counselor? At least I felt there was openness and understanding between us. But I have no idea what the future of her relation with this man is going to be. Would I do the same thing with another person in a similar situation that I did with her? I honestly don't know. And how about the parents? The ambiguity of this whole situation makes your head spin. There aren't any pat answers, and yet you have to take a stand somewhere. You can't just walk away from the problem; things like this are happening around us today all the time. In this case, I feel I can be most useful to the girl and her parents by being on hand if they need me. I hope I'm doing the right thing."

8. Whenever a person in emotional crisis is truly "opened," the counselor, too, is at least in some measure "opened" or reopened. Something happens that is hard to describe, except to say that neither one is quite the same as he used to be.

A well-intentioned but inexperienced counselor was consulted by a young unmarried woman who had a number of crippling fears. The counselor felt she was sexually inhibited and focused on this as the probable cause of her anxiety. She repeatedly told him with some anger that this kind of interpretation did not help her but simply made her feel more degraded.

It slowly dawned on the counselor that he was emphasizing negatives rather than positives, and that although she felt very inferior she actually had a high degree of courage and intelligence which he had underestimated. When he changed his emphasis to these qualities in her and became more encouraging, she improved considerably.

The last interview with her took place shortly before she was to be married. At the end of the interview both she and the counselor sensed the significance of the moment. She said to him, "It hardly seems possible that after all this time I won't be coming to see you." Then, with a little smile, she added, "What will you do without me?" The counselor's first reaction was to wonder whether she might be really saying, "What will I do without you?" But in the next instant he realized that her question was literally valid. He smiled and said, "I know what you mean. Whatever happens, I'm sure we'll always remember one another; and I don't think either of us will be quite the same as we were before. Somehow I like that idea. It seems very natural to me."

But now, after having considered the importance of "being opened" and the function of the pastoral counselor, someone may say that we have still not been specific enough as to just what the relationship is between "being opened" and an awareness of God's presence. When and how in the "opening" does one become aware of God? Or does one become aware of God at all? These are altogether fair questions which certainly deserve an opinion, if not an answer.

"Being opened" is not necessarily a single, complete, once-and-for-all phenomenon. There are various degrees of "being opened," and they are not all permanent. This was illustrated in the case of the man referred to earlier who during his illness was opened, but closed up again when he had recovered and went back to his old status quo. If one believes that it is God who really opens us, then the opening is bound to be incomplete unless we somehow recognize that God has brought it about. It is impossible to pinpoint when and how this recognition takes place. It may vary all the way from immediately to later, when the truth may gradually dawn.

The one thing that seems certain, as we have said before, is that the awareness of what God has done for us does not come to us in an unnatural or mystical way. It is a realization that not only have we found meaning in the midst of meaninglessness, and order in the midst of chaos, but also a very quiet conviction that somehow we have been led all along in a direction we were meant to go.[14] We cannot prove it, but we nevertheless believe it. One might say of it, "I can't explain why I believe this is so. All I know is that I just feel it in my bones. It goes as deep as that." Actually, it seems not so much a feeling as an understanding. One does not grasp it, but is grasped by it; and once that has happened, it persists and cannot be denied.[15]

---

[14] David A. MacLennan, *No Coward Soul* (New York: Oxford University Press, 1949), pp. 31–32.

[15] Karen L. Fink, "A Perspective on Healing in Pastoral Counseling" (dissertation submitted to Chicago Theological Seminary for B.D. degree 1968), p. 34.

V. "GO HOME TO YOUR FRIENDS, AND TELL THEM HOW MUCH THE LORD HAS DONE FOR YOU, AND HOW HE HAS HAD MERCY ON YOU (MARK 5:19, RSV)."

This is what Jesus told the man named Legion (Mark 5:19–20; Luke 8:38–39), from whom he had cast the devils out into the swine. The man in gratitude asked Jesus' permission to be allowed to accompany him. Here again, Jesus responded with a demand and a promise. The demand is to spread the word of God's good news *in the community*. Faith in God without an accompanying sense of community is unreal. The promise is that he has now become a *new man*.

Here is an aspect of pastoral counseling as essential as any of the others, which is probably the one most often overlooked. Many people in emotional crisis regard counseling as a process the goal of which is termination and the ability to go back to life much as it was before. This should not be the aim of pastoral counseling, particularly in view of what was said a little earlier in connection with "being opened." Although obviously, counseling sooner or later terminates, except in unusual situations, the true goal of pastoral counseling is not termination, but the beginning of a new way of life—the start of a growth process which hopefully will never stop. And it is kept going by the recognition of what God has done for one and gratitude for it.

One way of expressing gratitude to God is to do good works. A number of people have the misconception that doing good works constitutes a kind of insurance against personal crisis or disaster in the world. They see it as a means of being rewarded by God for good behavior. We mentioned before that this is not true "A free world is not a fair world," and misfortune afflicts the virtuous and evil doers alike. Among those who have pointed this out is Granger E. Westberg.[16]

He states that it is impossible for anyone to go directly to the kingdom of heaven and avoid misfortune, suffering, and despair simply by doing good works. In fact, this idea of good works is only a step away from the fallacy of self-sufficiency. It was shown earlier how a person who claims to be able to exist without God is more apt to experience emotional crisis. When we find ourselves unexpectedly in an emotional crisis, and perceive to our dismay that we are not self-sufficient after all, we may look to God or to our neighbor, including the pastoral counselor, for a miracle to save us. The pastoral counselor is an arm of God, but he cannot work miracles. It seems that God himself chooses not to work miracles as much as to rouse us gradually from self-concern, help us become aware of the possibilities within our reach, and guide us to what is right for us to do, often in such a quiet way that we may not realize at the time that we are being guided. What is right for us to do should be closely parallel to what we really want to do. A very telling instance of this is provided in *The Screwtape Letters* by the unhappy soul who said on his arrival in hell, "I now see that I spent most of my life in doing *neither* what I ought *nor* what I liked." [17] Such a life is sterile, indeed. Our

---

[16] From a personal communication.
[17] C. S. Lewis, *The Screwtape Letters* (New York: Macmillan, 1953), p. 64.

true mission is to do that which we both like and are equipped to do.

Is there anything we can say as to how we should go about doing good works? Obviously, this is to some extent a matter of individual preference, since there are so many different kinds of good works that people can do. But is not the most basic and essential way of doing good works the endeavor to fulfill our true mission in life as we have just defined it? It would seem that one of the necessary characteristics of the "beneficial presence" whom we have mentioned before must be that he is doing what he knows is right for him to do—what God has intended him to do—and that he enjoys doing it. This is one reason why it is such a happy, comforting, and even almost healing experience to be with this sort of person—some of his, or her, inner joy emanates and can be perceived by the other, who thereby becomes aware of hope and a possibility that he too may before long arrive at a state similar to this, in which through his personal contacts and through the way he lives he can pass the message on a little further.

The "beneficial presence" is certainly not immune to emotional crisis. No one is, even Jesus. The recognition of this is one thing that makes it possible for us to become a "beneficial presence" to others, in however small a way. Sometimes one may be a beneficial presence to others without having even been aware that this is what he or she has actually been.

It is through faith and trust that an emotional crisis can gradually be transformed into a constructive experience for the good, that can have lasting value. To the religious person, this means faith and trust in a higher power—God. The "neighbor," including the counselor, can never expect to be a substitute for God, but he may be very helpful in providing a means through which faith and trust in God can develop. Having passed through emotional crisis, it is all too easy to overlook, or to forget, or to render to some mortal, however beneficial he or she may have been, the gratitude that belongs truly to God. We can best express our gratitude to God by being open to his word, and to the needs of others, through carrying out to the utmost our task of doing what we should do, which is at the same time what we want to do. When we have, as we all sooner or later can have, the excitement of understanding what this is, then we are truly able to proclaim to others, "not only with our lips but in our lives," "how much the Lord has done."

APPENDIX A
PSYCHIATRY'S RESPONSIBILITY TO MEDICINE AND TO RELIGION*

Not long ago I was invited, as a psychiatrist, to be the discussion leader at a program for clergy on the subject of "mental illness." The program was centered around a speech by another psychiatrist on what the clergy can do to help emotionally disturbed people. The speech was well prepared and well delivered. The speaker believed sincerely that clergy and psychiatrists can and should work together. He told us that the relationship between the two is much friendlier now than it used to be. He particularly stressed the fact that the first person most people with emotional problems turn to is the clergyman. This, he thought, made sense.

He then said something that troubled me—the same thing I have heard at practically every meeting of this kind that I have attended. He made it clear that, whenever psychiatrist and clergyman work together to help people, the clergyman is considered to be essentially the junior partner. In my experience, the clergyman generally goes along with this idea. He regards the psychiatrist as the "expert" who is there to teach him how to recognize signs of "mental illness" and what

---

* This article by Dr. Howland is reprinted with permission from the *Chicago Theological Seminary Register*, 55 (1965), 1–4.

to do about it. What the psychiatrist most often teaches the clergyman is "not to get in over his head" and "when to refer."

Now these two points, of course, are of some importance. But they have been emphasized so strongly that a number of clergymen feel quite uneasy when counseling. They have gotten the impression that, compared to psychiatrists, clergymen are capable of doing only a superficial, second-rate hack job. They are so afraid of making mistakes that they are inclined to back away and give the emotionally upset person no guidance at all. This, I think, is not right either, and I question whether the whole relationship between psychiatrists and clergy can really be such a one-way street. But the possibility that the clergyman might have something to teach the psychiatrist does not seem to get much attention in these meetings.

When the speech was over, I met with my group and led the discussion. It would be more accurate to say that I conducted the discussion practically single-handed. The clergymen sat in a row, attentive but mute and deferential, almost like farm animals. I hoped they would loosen up and join in, but they never did.

Afterward, at lunch, I chanced to sit next to a minister I had met before. In the course of our conversation, I told him that I had been fortunate enough to be appointed psychiatric consultant to the counseling program of a large suburban church on the other side of Chicago and that my work there was expanding into what I thought might soon become a half-time position. The minister's eyes opened wide.

"Boy!" he exclaimed. "I wish we had something like that at my church. We need help terribly. Let me tell you about some of the people I'm counseling."

He did, and my own eyes opened—one very sticky marital problem; a woman with repeated illegitimate pregnancies; a person who sounded like a chronic psychotic; and there were others.

"Why, those are problems as tough as you will find in any psychiatrist's practice," I said.

"This isn't unusual," he answered. "People like this come to me all the time. I don't know what to do for them, but there is no one else I can send them to. Your office is too far away. [Unfortunately, that is true.] Besides, these are low-income families who can't afford to pay private fees. They work during the day, so they can't get into the psychiatric clinics because they are closed in the evening. I tried to work out some arrangement with the psychiatrists out my way, but they all say they are too busy. One of them was even recommended to me as being interested in working with clergy. But he couldn't have cared less when I talked to him. That means it's entirely up to me. I certainly want to help these people all I can, but I haven't had the training to know how to do it. All I'm doing with them is just hanging on. Sooner or later they are bound to wise up to this, and then they'll give up hope and fall completely apart."

This minister was not holding back now. The words were fairly bubbling out of him. I began to see the immensity of the problem.

"There must be many ministers in the same fix as you," I said.

"Yes, there are," he replied quickly.

I have often thought about my conversation with that minister. I am convinced that we psychiatrists do not fully understand what the nature and extent of our responsibility to the clergy really are. The point to remember is that, although the psychiatrist is usually considered the "expert," most people seeking help go to the clergyman first. The clergyman, however, frequently does not feel prepared for this. As a theological student he gets very little supervised experience in counseling. There are postgraduate training courses in pastoral counseling—and some of them are good—but for practical reasons of time and money they are beyond the reach of the average parish clergyman. It is small wonder, therefore, that clergymen feel inadequate and shaky when people come to them with emotional problems. I do not think that it is too helpful to keep telling them not to get in over their heads, when a lot of them are in over their heads already for the simple reason that there is nothing else they can do. They have no access to a psychiatrist; they are on their own.

This is where the clergyman needs the psychiatrist. Now, does the psychiatrist need the clergyman? I believe he does.

Why is it that people with problems pick the clergyman more often than the psychiatrist? There are three main reasons, as I see it. Two are obvious because they are also practical—the clergyman is cheaper and he is usually more accessible. Psychiatrists are fewer and harder to find.

But there is another reason that seems to me to be very important: *people fear the psychiatrist far more than they do the clergyman.* There are, of course, some individual exceptions, but generally this is true. There is a sharp contrast between the popular image of the psychiatrist as the expert who is best qualified to help and the actual fact that the majority of people are afraid to go to him. Certain public attitudes toward psychiatry have not changed. One very common reaction is that "if you go to a psychiatrist, it means that you are nuts." "Mentally sick" is assumed to be merely a synonym for "crazy." In spite of everything psychiatrists have said to the contrary, the idea persists that psychiatry deals essentially with crazy people.

There is still a widespread general impression of something unnatural and "spooky" about psychiatry—an impression of strange jargon and mysterious trappings and rituals, especially the couch. It is remarkable how many laymen have no concept of psychiatry other than of something that happens on a couch. At a party where I was introduced to fifty people, forty-six—I counted—immediately made some facetious remark to me about the couch. People have a tendency to identify and confuse the couch with the actual treatment process. It all sounds queer to them, and they do not want any part of it. Actually, whether or not a psychiatrist uses a couch is largely a matter of his personal preference. Some psychiatrists think talking face to face is just as effective and more natural.

The most extreme instance of the fear of psychiatry is the claim of some right-wing groups in this country that psychiatry is part of a Communist plot to overthrow our government by brainwashing. This claim is curiously persistent. Psychiatrists naturally deny it, as they should. But I cannot remember hearing the question raised as to how it is possible for such a preposterous idea to be believed at all. The answer, I feel, is that, in spite of all the publicity psychiatry has received, *people still do not understand what psychiatry really is or what psychiatrists really do.* I have a growing suspicion that this may be because we psychiatrists ourselves do not understand.

What is psychiatry? We are taught to think of it chiefly as a medical science concerned with "diagnosis" and "cure" of "diseases" (that is, "diseases of the mind"). There is no question that psychiatry and medicine are *related* to each other. We do not need to go into that. The trouble comes when we are tempted to treat psychiatry as if it were *identical* with medical science. It is not. It cannot be scientifically validated. Most psychiatrists know this. They readily admit that it is impossible to prove beyond a doubt that psychiatry has ever helped anybody—though we assume it probably has. Psychiatrists cannot agree on what the criteria of a "cure" are, or what constitutes "mental illness," and some even wonder how accurate the term "mental illness" is. Of course, neurophysiology and neuropharmacology, which have some bearing on psychiatry, are sciences, but that is quite a different matter. Most of psychotherapy, or counseling, in its present state cannot be called a science.

Here is something else. Psychiatric teaching really begins with some scheme of "normal" personality development. This is divided into stages, presented in chronological order from birth through childhood and adolescence to "maturity" and aging. The problems a person may meet in each of these stages are pointed out. Now the logical place for any such scheme of development to end would be in death. It is very interesting, however, that none of them do. They all end in old age. Death as an entity is not taken up in detail. Psychiatry does not seem to have recognized death as a fundamental part of the scheme of life.

The psychiatrist may say he is not qualified to discuss the meaning of death, because this is a philosophical and not a scientific or even psychiatric question. But I feel it is very much a psychiatric question. Death is not something vague, hanging somewhere off in the distance, beyond old age. Death is a stark reality that can and does happen at any time of life, including the very beginning. The only thing that we all have in common is our mortality. *It is the most basic determinant of human behavior.* Is not this, then, a psychiatric question?

In Freud's time emotional disorders were blamed on sex. Later the feeling was that anger and dependence were responsible. To be sure, all of these are still factors, but I suspect that beneath them is a deeper fear rooted in a realization that man is mortal and therefore cannot control his own destiny in the way he would like to. His hopes and plans can be interrupted without any warning. I find that the response of many people to this realization is either to withdraw from living or to try harder and harder to control what they know all the while is beyond their control—people, things, even their world. Neither of these ways works. Those who are involved just feel more anxious.

Contemporary psychiatry tries to help them by means of a better self-understanding. But in the search for self-understanding, psychiatry runs the risk of making people simply more self-concerned and self-preoccupied. *It tends to turn people inward when what they really need is to turn outward.* They need to understand what they can do and what they cannot and then do what they can and leave the rest alone. A few have managed to do this by sheer blind courage. But, for most people, that is not enough. They need some sort of faith. It is at this point that the psychiatrist can learn from the clergyman. They are both involved, and the problem is a spiritual one.

A number of people think of religion and psychiatry as two entirely different enterprises. I see psychiatry, however, as having fundamentally a religious task, and one of its big troubles, I think, is that it does not recognize this.

It is no secret that many psychiatrists realize that psychiatry has serious shortcomings. My own feelings about it are:

1. *It is not economically sound.*—It is still something mainly for the relatively well-to-do. Low-cost clinics have not solved the problem. The clergyman and the doctor take care of most emotionally upset people.
2. *It is not professionally sound.*—People are afraid of it because they cannot understand it. It tries to be a science when it is not, and it overlooks the fact that it is closely linked not only to medicine but to religion. This oversight has created tremendous confusion.

As a psychiatrist, I do not intend to be unfair to my profession. The mistakes it has made are honest ones. I do, however, have a suggestion for the correction of each of these two deficiencies.

1. The psychiatrist should spend more time in training the clergyman and the family doctor to carry the major part of the load, which I am sure they will continue doing.
2. The psychiatrist should take more initiative in working actively with the clergyman in the development of pastoral counseling, paying particular attention to the unique position of the clergyman as a minister of God and how this can be used to greatest advantage in helping troubled people.

If these things should come about, my hunch would be that clergy and family doctors would carry even more of the load with relative comfort, while psychiatrists would gradually function more as supervisors and consultants than as therapists, and that in time there might even be fewer psychiatrists needed. Since I am convinced that emotional problems have spiritual dimensions, I am particularly impressed by the potentialities of the pastoral counselor. The psychiatrist could perform a great service by helping to give this man the proper training.

APPENDIX B

THE CLERGYMAN'S UNIQUE CONTRIBUTION TO HEALTH*

The clergyman about to be told of his unique contributions to health, I suspect, may be not only pleased but also a bit puzzled. I know of no one who is the recipient of so much conflicting advice and opinion as the clergyman. On the one hand, he is commended for his "unique contributions" and on the other hand he hears that God is dead and that religion has become irrelevant in our time. He has often been warned against being "judgmental" and "throwing the Bible" at people who come to him for counseling, but on the other hand he is now confronted with the statement that the clergy have abdicated their claim to moral competence so that the psychotherapist must take over as the moral arbitrator.[1] He is told "not to get over his head" and "when to refer" without consideration of the fact that there is often no one to whom he can re-

---

* Read at the annual meeting of the Academy of Religion and Mental Health, Chicago, Illinois, April 26, 1966. This article by Dr. Howland is reprinted with permission from *The Journal of Pastoral Care*, 21 (1967), 91–93.

[1] P. London: *The Modes and Morals of Psychotherapy*; Holt, Rinehart, and Winston, New York, 1964.

fer so that he has no choice but to be over his head.[2] The one unquestionable piece of truth he knows is that most people with emotional problems come first to him; and he feels ill-prepared to help them.

Now I believe the clergyman has indeed a unique contribution to make to health by virtue of his position as a representative of God. But to understand what this contribution is, it is important for us to be sure what we mean by "health." "Health" actually has two meanings. This is possible because the words "health," "whole," and "holy" all come from the same root. "Health" may be used in the narrower sense of physical or medical health, which is the doctor's concept. But it may also be used in the broader sense of the "whole man," who has a spiritual as well as a physical dimension. This is the clergyman's concept. Confusion has arisen because we are not careful to specify which meaning of "health" we are talking about. The broader meaning is often implied when closer examination shows that one is actually using the narrower meaning.

An outstanding example of this is the concept of "mental health." The implication is usually that by "mental health" we mean the broader view of the "whole man." But if we consider the criteria of "mental health" as ordinarily presented, we find this is not so. These criteria are: (1) Being free from symptoms. (2) Being unhampered by emotional conflict. (3) Having a reasonable work capacity. (4) Being able to have

---

[2] E. S. Howland, "Psychiatry's Responsibilitiy to Medicine and to Religion," *Chicago Theological Seminary Register*, 15 (Feb. 1965), 1–4.

meaningful relationships with others. (5) Lately "spiritual health" has been added to the other four, but generally as follows: "A sound religious belief can be one factor contributing to mental health."

In the first place, it is evident that all these criteria are entirely secular, including "spiritual health," because it has been subordinated to "mental health." Hence there is really no spiritual dimension whatever in this concept. Moreover, if we consider the first two of these criteria, it appears that a "healthy" person is not expected even to *have* symptoms—for example, anxiety or depression—let alone be hampered by them. One might well ask whether such criteria are compatible with religious commitment, in which there may be confrontation with truth that may make one not only anxious but even temporarily less effective in his usual tasks.

Two questions then arise: (1) If these are the aims of "mental health," are they adequate for a member of any religious faith? (2) Are these the aims which the clergy should be promoting? Personally I would answer "no" to both questions. Furthermore, I do not see how the clergyman can possibly make a unique contribution in this particular frame of reference—that is, as a "mental health worker."

The misunderstanding that results from trying to make the clergyman into a "mental health worker" is further illustrated by certain aspects of the relationship between religion and psychiatry. Several claims are generally made about this relationship: that it is much better than it used to be, that there is more dialogue between the two professions, and that "competent members of both professions behave responsibly toward each other."[3] My own experience as a psychiatrist who has attended a number of interdisciplinary meetings and participated in some is that these claims are not valid. I am aware instead of attempts to get the two professions together, and a wish that has become practically a determination to believe that the relationship is better—but I do not think it really is. I find a careful interdisciplinary politeness but hardly any real dialogue, and very little truly responsible behavior between the two professions. Indeed, I doubt that either profession understands what its responsibility to the other actually is. Too often there is the familiar "one-way street" along which the psychiatrist leads the clergyman. Here again I feel that this is an instance where the narrower "medical" view of health prevails.

According to this narrower view of health, anxiety and depression are usually "neurotic," unrealistic, and therefore symptoms of illness. The suggested remedy is to try to come to grips with significant incidents in the past. This involves turning *inward*. The psychiatrist seeks not to change an individual's value system, but to produce an inner harmony within the existing one. When this occurs, he says a "cure" has been accomplished, implying that a process has thereby terminated.

With the broader view of health, however, things are altogether different. Anxiety and depression are seen, not as alien symptoms, but as normal reactions to the awareness of our finitude and relative helpless-

---

[3] E. Draper: *Psychiatry and Pastoral Care*; Prentice-Hall, Englewood Cliffs, New Jersey, 1965.

ness in the universe. What is needed here is to come to grips with one's responsibility in the present—hence, to turn outward and not inward. Turning outward involves leaving alone what one cannot control, including his anxiety and depression, and living fully while he can. This necessitates trust, which puts us on religious ground,[4] because such trust goes beyond simple trust in the counselor. With this viewpoint, some change in the person's value system would seem inevitable, and the goal is not a "cure" but rather an experience in religious education, which implies that a process has not terminated but begun. Even when he no longer sees the counselor, the individual will continue turning outward and growing responsibly in the world and in the fellowship of believers.

The unique contribution, as I see it, of the clergyman to health is to foster not "mental health," which is a shallow and secular concept, but trustful responsibility in a religious sense, which is his proper job. In order to do this he should be trained not as a "mental health worker" but as a pastoral counselor. One person who may be able to help train the clergyman as a pastoral counselor is the psychiatrist, but only if he sees the necessity of a reorientation for himself, and an awareness of a spiritual dimension which until now he has not realized is any of his business. As this awareness comes about, real dialogue between the two professions will become possible.

---

[4] E. S. Howland, "Psychiatry's Responsibility to Medicine and to Religion," *Bulletin of The Johns Hopkins Hospital*, 117 (Sept. 1965), 137–39.